Why We Need Arts Education

D1809172

Why We Need Arts Education

Revealing the Common Good: Making Theory and Practice Work Better

Howard Cannatella

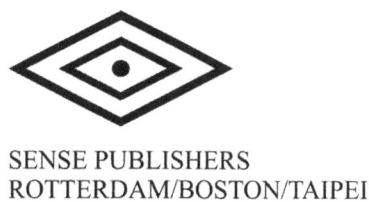

SENSE PUBLISHERS
ROTTERDAM/BOSTON/TAIPEI

A C.I.P. record for this book is available from the Library of Congress.

ISBN: 978-94-6300-092-5 (paperback)
ISBN: 978-94-6300-093-2 (hardback)
ISBN: 978-94-6300-094-9 (e-book)

Published by: Sense Publishers,
P.O. Box 21858,
3001 AW Rotterdam,
The Netherlands
https://www.sensepublishers.com/

Printed on acid-free paper

All Rights Reserved © 2015 Sense Publishers

No part of this work may be reproduced, stored in a retrieval system, or transmitted in any form or by any means, electronic, mechanical, photocopying, microfilming, recording or otherwise, without written permission from the Publisher, with the exception of any material supplied specifically for the purpose of being entered and executed on a computer system, for exclusive use by the purchaser of the work.

TABLE OF CONTENTS

INTRODUCTION

Two yards of politeness do not make society for me.

Henry David Thoreau (2009, p. 328)

Art is an experience of awe and solace. Successive societies have viewed art as a significant source of pleasure and critical judgement. In order to show that art reflects our imagination, feeling, cognition, perception, culture and experience, what must it do? Of common unanimity it must represent the character of existence that is near to an equality of actual life. We only need to read Homer's *Illiad* or visit the Louvre in Paris to unflinchingly acknowledge that art is fitted to this purpose. It is anachronistic to think otherwise. The customary feelings of delight and adoration accompanying the art experience when reading Homer's *Illiad* or visiting the Louvre raises our spirits and reflects our consciousness and desires. Our entire personality and our entire feeling and thinking of the indivdiual and society, the landscape and the lives that people lead is what art expresses. Crafted objects, theatre performances, festivals, state buildings, museums, concert halls, films, public art exhibitions, and frequent visits to one's public library, suggest that art is socially beneficial. So much is crammed into so little when the poet Herbert Zbigniew sagaciously mentions of the Paleolithic Lascaux Cave paintings that no greatness in life can be separated from its support (Herbert, 1985, p. 17). As Arthur Schopenhauer (1995) suggests, art produces definite grades of our reality of the world. Moreover, of supporting relevance to the case I am going to make, is the unmistakeable fact that the arts have always been able to produce a glittering pedigree of constructive insights, experienced as "uplifting, redeeming and reconciling" (Küng, 1981, p. 27) productions which, as I have begun to imply, are of immense ethical importance, the way the arts perpetuate, enrich and transform the common good in life. Haida culture, in a variety of ways, has always drawn on the service of art as a common good. Other contemplations of the common good of art in life relates further to epoch radical producing works: Monteverdi's *Vespers* 1610, Bach's *St Matthew Passion* 1727, Rembrandt's *The Anatomy Lesson of Dr. Nicolaes Tulp* 1661, Kafka's *The Metamorphosis* 1915, the choreographer George Balanchine (1902–83), Mondrian's *Composition with Line (Pier and Ocean)* 1917, Duchamp's *Fountain* 1917 and Picasso's *Guernica* 1937. Not forgetting the accompaniment of more humble works of art that are just as important a commitment to the common good in life: Jan Frans Dael's *Vase of Flowers, Grapes and Peaches* 1810, Samuel Palmer's *A Cornfield by Moonlight with the Evening Star* 1830, Hans Christian Anderson's *The Ugly Duckling* 1844, Mary Cassatt's *The Bath* 1891–2, Carl Larsson's *Hide-and-Seek* 1900, Laura Knight's *Ruby Loftus Screwing a Breech Ring* 1943, and Louisa Mary Alcott's *Little Women* 1868–69. Hence we can say that the value of art, as Hans Küng undisputably points out, ought be seen "against a nihilistic background" (Küng, 1981, p. 29) of inhumanity of being in the world.

However, we can trace back opposition to the value of art in society, which continues to this day, to Plato. Wise as Plato was, I view as unforgiveable, the reductionist manner that cleverly enabled him to mock with marvelous, inartistic, overpowering skill an art's human affirmation and interpretation of the world (Nietzsche, 1968). Narrow-mindedly, Plato dupes us into believing that Homer and the other noted poets that he mentions in his *Republic* (1997) lead us astray. This would not matter so much if education came right out and dissociated itself from Plato's thinking about art; if it stood behind its lectern with its written notes to explain why art education is of tremendous relevance to education in general.

The triumph of art in society comes from community demands for it that have noticed how art can promote improvements in life due to what is learnt from art. Our attraction to art comes from the performances, tones, pitches, rhythms, evocations, gestures, images, forms, shapes, reasons, pathos, sentiments, visions, voices, ideas and articulations of an art that concomitantly represent different, compassionate, public interests of life. Anthony Storr (1992, p. 1–4) states accurately that the arts enhance our feeling of personal worth, that they enable us to comprehend ourselves and our external world in ways that touch the core of our physical, emotional and mental being, temporarily transforming our whole existance befitting of intense and common, pleasureably, shared experiences that concomittently increase our capacity for dealing effectively with social tasks and relationships which make up our lives.

To substantially value art requires access to the teaching of it in education. Access to art education was made possible by the world of art, by universal literacy in society, by on-going democratic political reforms, by meeting industrial, commercial and social economic demands and by the unveiling of a public school system of education during the nineteenth century (Efland, 1990), driving access to art education that became widespread after the Second World War.

There have been considerable improvements in pedagogical curriculum design thinking, teaching methods, school choices and professionalization standards that have driven more regulated, operational and accountable systems in education since the Second World War. These changes owe much to Dewey's 1916 monumental work *Democracy and Education* (1944). Yet we seem to be going backwards not forwards for art was once a revered traditional subject but it is not anymore. Access to any reasonable instruction of an art continues to vary enormously from school-to-school, district-to-district, city-to-city, state-to-state and from country-to-country. Citing research from the Associated Board of the Royal Schools of Music (ABRSM, 2014), the concert pianist James Rhodes, in a letter to a national newspaper in 2014, mentions how children from disadvantaged backgrounds face enormous inequality in accessing music education. In the National Society for Education in Art and Design Survey Report (2014), its findings seem to mirror what Elliot Eisner (2005), in early published work noted, that art, craft and design education in the US was a negligible subject in a school's curriculum. Inequality was also an issue that the President's

Committee on the Arts and the Humanities (2011), recognised in relation to access to the arts. This report also mentions that the "arts in schools are on a downward trend", finding that federal and state governments should abandon the current policy of "allowing" the arts as an expenditure of a comprehensive educational system in favour of giving them a more robust place in it on the premise that the nation's capability requires a workforce that is resourceful, inventive and creative which is best fostered through the arts. The call for arts education is not just coming from the arts; science disciplines such as medical education are calling for student doctors to have some formal education in the arts (medical humanities) believing that doctors need a comprehensive education to enable them to become better doctors (Batistatou, 2010; Gordon, 2005).

One might conclude that a watershed has been reached about the beneficial effects of what art education in a public system of education contributes. The arts help us understand our social and personal lives better. Society, having made so many social advances through the arts, is globally recapitulating today, drawing back from this culture and student's educational access to it. Should we be outraged that art which is founded on human affairs, common life and conversation is being woefully ignored in education? Is art not a model that is dependent upon peoples' conditions and experiences? Suffice to say that the misfortunes of anyone's education is not to have realised the social importance of art and how art, makes us feel. Dismissive we have become of finer things. How art makes us feel shouldn't be taken lightly bearing in mind how much it can affect our human conduct in the world. It seems sensible to recognise how near to perfection art expresses being in the world and doesn't this make it educationally an important issue? Good and evil and everything in-between consisting of: vanity, vehemence, ugliness, ignorance, hatred, insensitivity, snobbery, sorrow, uneasiness, compassion, kindness, softness, hardness, transparency, calmness, soothingness, joyfulness, cheerfulness, beauty, love, excitement, fun, nature, relaxation, delicacy, melody, mellowness, wonder, grace, colour, eloquence, drama, play, concern, helpfulness, reassurance, peacefulness, puzzlement, coldness, fragility, brokenness, bitterness, boldness, greed, boastfulness, rudeness, industry, fright, incredulity, fancifulness, flirtatiousness, misogyny, reclusivity, determinedness, cleverness, criticism, subtlty, murkiness, unluckiness, reliability, pathos, decadence, death, birth, braveness, poverty, observance, regretfulness, selfishness, idleness, foolishness, destruction, power, passion, fractiousness, malfeasance, and calamity, for example, are the spectacles of art communication.

Art education should concern us all because art education can drive up standards in education and be central to them. It is this proposition that I intend to examine. Art education, Martha Nussbaum suggests, is "reading for life". Quoting Charles Dickens, Nussbaum (1990, p. 230) mentions that when beaten by his stepfather and cut off from the love and care of his mother, David Copperfield finds himself sitting on a bed reading as if for life. Not so different from this is how John Stuart Mill in his autobiography explains briefly how art transformed, enlightened and saved him from a zombie like existence of living, made him feel more human and sympathetic to the world. The arts, David Hume (1965, p. 27) argues correctly, "draw off the mind from the hurry of business". Are we being therefore hoodwinked into believing wrongly that subjective experiences, as Mary Midgley (2014) argues, are becoming an irrelevance to being in the world turning "to check the sallies of the imagination and reduce every expression to geometric truth and exactness" (Hume, 1965, p. 7), which as David Hume goes on to comment further, in his 1757 essay *Of the Standard of Taste*, makes art insipid, negating the many circumstances to be compared in existance when "our judgement will be strengthen by this exercise. We shall form juster notions of life" (Hume, 1965, p. 27).

I am going to address why we should be teaching art education more comprehensively in our public system of education and how should we be doing this. While a patchy educational delivery of art education and the accompanying embarrassing, infrequent timetable arrangements for teaching art (Eisner, 2005) is hardly helpful to demonstrating what art in education could achieve, this in itself is not a good enough reason for teaching art in an extended way in education. But a good reason why art education should be extended in education would be a pedagogy of teaching art that pays much more attention to the moral good of art education for life.

Productions and discussions about art can focus on self-centred, self-serving demands. For example, in teaching 'the virtues of ambiguity in art' or in teaching the skills of a particular art, these concerns can ignore the more substantial educational view of art that says that art education, because it is intended for society, ought to be able to enlarge our common understanding that is part of our humanity, of our shared existence in the world expressing life's social aesthetic pleasures. The autonomy of art is also not a convincing reason why we should teach art to a reasonable degree in a public system of education. However good a five-star programme of art education in this school, college or university is consistently rated, a public system of education supporting a faculty of art in education along art-for-arts-sake curriculum lines, for instance, would be seen clearly as too narrow a domain for a public education system to ambitiously support. In the melting pot of art creation, autonomy is vital, but society is never appreciative of art production and performances until such art shows itself anchored in human associations of social life. Art achievement and its value have to contribute to the common good in the same way that science, maths and business must do. The role of art education is to show how valuable art is to society.

Currently, various art educational groups, educational professionals in general and various practicing artists and art societies work well together as a unit overseeing the curriculum of art, where there has been a continuing view of art education with much merit to it that has focused on discipline-based, free-expression, and more artists and industry in schools and colleges, for example, as one set of on-going art educational reforms. Other reforms that impact just as importantly on art education are arts' curriculum design thinking, pedagogical standards, criteria led outcomes, benchmarks, cognitive and social psychological development theories, ethical commitments, administrative procedures, academic reports, teaching inspections, parent-teacher committees, governing bodies, and data collection statistical processes.

The teaching of art in education involves a material, text, activity and form-focused, fixed attention and discriminatory approach. Key ideas and conceptions of art, skill based exercises, discipline-based, knowledge based and critical, cultural and contextual thinking can be found in lots of art curriculum design plans, together with self-directed, experimenting, experiential, subject-specific, workshop, theatre, performance and studio based tasks, exercise and projects of art. To teach art well in education, also requires an understanding of student learning at elementary, high-school or college-university levels of public education. A diagnostic approach which is student-centered and which involves case studies in art teaching, special needs teaching, classroom management and skills, organization, processes and methods, assessment strategies, external assessor's involvement, lesson planning, curriculum understanding, school visits and visiting performers, such as speakers, poets, ceramists and painters, substantively qualify what constitutes art education.

Such is my contention that although art education is designed to stimulate students' productive, creative, discerning and rewarding reflections of art and life in learner-like social ways that are good for society overall, it is a claim neither sufficiently appreciated by education thinking in the round nor steered adequately in art education. Art education, through a social approach, needs more emphasizing in order to have a greater affect on public education. The continuous, developing and regular instruction of art in education and the pursuit of its legitimacy requires a good account of its social relevance and pedagogy. Art in education would benefit from more socially reconstructed enriching programmes of art in order to address the fact that there is little public awareness of the collective reasons why art education should be seen as essential. Until this situation changes, art education will continue to be sidelined.

This book is an attempt to paint a social picture of what art education offers society. Our culture acknowledges that art education is a part of our human understanding in the world, but pitifully rather sees it today, as Hegel (1988) predicted in his *Aesthetics,* as no longer a substantial and essential experience of life, no longer erudite and touching in its majesty. Perhaps it should be borne in mind, however, how deeply we cultivate and judge things that are amazing, exciting, beautiful, pleasurable, of human skill, of our spirit, redeeming, concerned with human relationships, sensitive and of being in the world, which in human form, art in education explicates. Construing, recognizing, transforming, creating and elucidating our conceptions and experiences of life through art education notably in literature, poetry, dance, music, theatre, fashion, textiles, design, architecture, crafts, film, photography, sculpture and painting, for example, involves our human sympathetic feelings. By paying greater attention to the multitude of diverse creative ways art education expresses the social and insisting that it primarily does so, makes our world and art education all the better. The demise of art education leads to the demise of human happiness.

UTILITY

The Happiness Principle

Only the most superficial of people "could fail to realise what impressionism, fauvism, and expressionism, what cubism, futurism, constructivism, as well as dada and surrealism, have discovered for us by way of new horizons, bestowed on us by way of wealth of invention, revealed to us by way of bold experiment."

(Küng, 1981, p. 18)

Without fear of contradiction, John Stuart Mill (1806–73) is acknowledged as an exceptional philosopher, political scientist, educationalist, social reformer and art lover. As a Utilitarian, Mill believed that human happiness involved the principle of utility. Utilitarianism is a theory that sets out to give an account of the permanent cause of our common and social human happiness in the world and of what stands in its way in terms of pain (Mill, 2007, p. 6–7). I am interested in exploring in a basic manner, one particular view of Utilitarianism. It is Mill's utilitarian thinking involving the idea: "that our own lives and the institutions of society should be such that welfare overall is maximised" (Crisp, 1997, p. 173) expressing the "principle of utility, or as Bentham latterly called it, the great happiness principle" (Mill, 2007, p. 3). Utilitarianism was a new, radical, social, philosophical concept, progressive in its thinking and just what the world needed, as it illustrated the indispensible condition that welfare maximization overall was important for human happiness. Not enough attention is paid to this concern in art education.

I am going to apply this utilitarian claim of how we should live, being informed, as Mill suggests, by what art in education can offer as a capacity capable of confirming our communal life promoting as examples our human happiness in the world for everyone overall. Which means that art education programmes need to reflect and express the continuing commonest experiences of life that enable society to feel the verity of art accomplishment in welfare maximization overall satisfying ways. Mill's utilitarian thinking involves why the arts, and therefore education about the arts, need cultivating in society, as he believed that this was a cause and a preserve of our common social human happiness.

What constitutes human happiness is the quality of life we experience and in association the quality of art we embrace knowing what the beneficence of an art educational experience means as a component of welfare maximisation overall. To reiterate, art education has to be able to substantiate and explain superiorly how art

1

activity and experiences adds to the quality of human life socially. This work in its entirety is an attempt to address these concerns.

For Mill, human happiness must benefit from art education and that means knowing what art education can contribute, how it is and why it is a suitable and meaningful experience for enjoying things that relate to the common good in life. Mill believed that the 'great happiness principle' affects and is affected by welfare maximisation overall and that art education was a vital part of the 'great happiness principle' because aesthetic life was one of the 'higher qualities' of human understanding that Mill noted was required in society for community happiness and its advancement. Mill surmises that the worth of an art's education is related to how secure, capable, learner-like enabling and how valuable the higher qualities of art's aesthetic education (involving intellectual, moral, social and sympathetic human feelings) contribute to the pleasure of the common good in life, not just momentarily but in longevity. What is taught should be useful throughout life, stay with us and be a constant source of pleasure and understanding. Education has overlooked how the arts in education are able to inculcate by fine strokes important, sensible touches of social life. This can be confirmed by how arts displays itself in common life. How art softens our passions, infuses and energizes our feelings, thoughts, ideas and imagination, arouses our interests and conversations, nourishes our attentions and pleasures, enlightens the mind about injustices, disgust, beauty and love, entertains the public, brings communities together through touching performances and representations, preserves continuity and change in life and creates admirable objects and buildings. The depth and extent of an art's history, the current practices of art and developmental teaching approaches in an art's education, were for Mill, indispensible signs of how art activity and experience can facilitate human happiness. We take for granted the relevance of art when arguably we should not. Taking out of context something Hume mentions that relates to Mill's way of thinking about the role of art in education is how art is "the conversational world joined to a social disposition and a taste for pleasure" (Hume, 1965, p. 38), showing such refinement that must have involved various exercises and discussions in education along the way, directing improvement through variety accustomed to common learning experiences that open pertinently the students' eyes, ears and thoughts of positive status, shaken, mixed and stirred and staying with them informatively and joyfully throughout the student-adult life.

If we are to be convinced of this, Mill argues that definite and indefinite progressive improvements in an art's education must perpetually deliver the distinctions, know-how and experiences of art that have a cumulative, consistent and regular effect on human happiness in socially agreed, intelligent ways. An art's education, Mill thought, has to be teaching, examining and testing actions, activities, skills, ideas, concepts, knowledge and student's experiences, in order for progression of the form-making, concept-making higher qualities of an art to shed light insightfully on human happiness. Mill also mentions that human happiness has to be free of pain but this does not mean that art is not a painful experience, as a tragedy can be, for example, but rather that art must not be harmful to social well-being. Since aesthetic life affects the 'great happiness principle' teaching art has to be bound in pedagogically, instrumental ways to the notion of welfare maximization overall. I am going to extrapolate how the pedagogy of art education conjoined to our aesthetic human life facilitates the conception of this higher quality that Mill sees is an aspect of welfare maximization overall.

Teaching art in education implies that the teaching of art is incrementally related to advancing the higher qualities of a curriculum of art in education but, equally in teaching and learning the higher qualities of an art practice are also in turn promoting welfare maximisation overall conjoined to the 'great happiness principle'. Teachers of art, the general public, educational policy makers and politicians need reassurance that the value of art education advances the 'higher qualities' of an art, favourably and readily serves the common good in life. How this is to be achieved, I have started to explain. Mill believed that art activity plays an active role in the quality of life in the world that hitherto maximizes human happiness overall. For the pleasure taken from an art production, he argued, can promote great joy, consolation and beauty that in commonly agreed cultural ways cements the role of art in society. Aristotle, Kant, Hegel, Hume, Mill, John Dewey, Iris Murdoch and Martha Nussbaum, for example, have stated that art activity is a mark of good character when touched by the common occurances of life, of the soundest judgements improving our sensibility having taken a higher interest in life's pleasurable, moral, social, intellectual and practical concerns.

In his art papers, in his autobiography and in extracts of other published works of his, Mill expounds how art plays an active role in the quality of life that hitherto facilitates maximisation of human happiness overall. For the pleasure taken from an art production, Mill claimed, could enter into the spirit of a person's character, attitudes, intellect and their concerns of fair play and justice in the world. Such a production could promote reasonable conceptions of wrecked, tormented or mischievous lives, of the virtues people display, of the relieving experience of an art, the affirmation, negation and synthesis of irrepressible and surprising common feelings for life, of things serene, attractive, celebrated, simple and grand, reviving life's being in the world, encouraging cheerfulness and human happiness. The merits of discussing, for example, in a class of how Achilles in Homer's *Iliad* shows prudence, love, courage, ferocity, cunning and obsession. Such humanity we applaud because of the plausible and realistic account of Homer's narrative that correspondingly conveys what is beneficial to discuss; of art adapted to life. A student's self-consciousness of art in education, can heighten and elevate their thoughts in experience, drawing attention to issues that can affect their social and personal existence, arousing feelings of security, energy, insight, and obligation that aptly affects their ideas, affections, beliefs and properties and character of their own art production work. To read some of the novels of Victor Hugo, Charles Dickens, Emile Zola, John Steinbeck, Charlotte Brontë and Margaret Drabble, for example, is surely to realise and compare how the superior intelligence of such writing is adapted justly to the power of sympathizing with certain human beings as generally portrayed in self-

3

regarding ways in these novels, which can then arouse our own feelings sufficiently to strengthen our own social-obligations (Mill, 2007, p. 44). Key thoughts in Mill's philosophy of human happiness are safety, equality, liberty, commonality, superior qualities and fraternity. To read Harper Lee's *To Kill a Mockingbird* and be moved by it is advantageous to society.

Art, Mill surmised, can encourage the loving character of a person to blossom or unburden their problems when grasping the conception of an object or scene that makes them laugh or through the quality of an unselfish act of moral commitment portrayed through an art performance that people experience cathartically. By noticing the moonlight, the milking of a cow, a knitting bag in a figure's hand and a snowflake on the window pane that answers to understanding, meaning and joy for the way in which the art work portrays such objects as a source of an aesthetic appreciation that reminds us of our everyday pleasures. An art production can lift one's burden, enabling us to see and feel relaxed; enjoying the self-consoling fantasy experience presented in J.M. Barrie's *Peter Pan*, for example, a forgetfulness of ourselves and our selfishness too. Where else in an educational curriculum is there a "leading back of thought to belief in spirit" (Croce, 1968, p. xxiii)?

Art experiences, Mill certainly asserted, can as explained, provide reassurance, resolve, and heighten human existence in the world in order to perceive, calculate, please, disturb and instruct common things about the world. It is the higher qualities of an art activity expressing musically, theatrically, in dance and in poetry, for example, that can cement our human associations, perceive painful and pleasurable human experiences of life that cohere with our own thoughts that can convince us of our delights and human failings. Mill surmises that the value of art performances and productions are in proportion to how they attract our intense feelings, cogitations, imagination and human sympathies actualising desires and needs that are closer to our own thoughts. Art production creates vivid conceptions that can be imaginatively perceived in different ways to give the attached incidents of a life that in seeing it, hearing it and in reading it we can reflect what we have learnt from it. Mill saw that quality in art has to relate to life's higher aesthetic sensibilities, conceptions and feelings that express human happiness, displaying and explaining what generates its satisfactory possession as being good for us and what hinders its acceptance due to the meaness, confusion, ignorance, insensitivity and prejudice of life, for example. He saw higher aesthetic concerns as essential to furthering welfare maximisation overall and the 'great happiness principle'.

When a student gets excited in an art class it can be a relief to their mind to find out that other students in the art class share similar feelings about the art exercise. A class can have in common their own self-consciousness of the world that in turn can stimulate elevated thoughts arousing correspondingly their happiness and admiration as the features and qualities of a student art performance or production are created to make outward impressions vivid, distinct and meaningful.

Cognition, being obviously important for human happiness, has considerable bearing on the quality of the student's enjoyment conjoined to the art work's value and understanding. Students are encouraged in education to see, imagine and hear loving characters in a novel, or something in the art's representation that enables them to forget as previously mentioned their own personal problems through the expressed laughable scenes, jocund voices, connected catharsisism and of the self-realised quality of an unselfish act portrayed in a drama. An art experience becomes a source of energy taken from the art activity that lifts the students' spirits in ways that they can return to see more of it and do more with it, a self-consoling experience of letting be in order to reveal, as Heidegger (1993) mentions in his *The Origin of the Work of Art*, thinking which gives way to unmasking, unearthing, imparting and telling, of what an art teacher would be interested in.

Without being explicit, Mill indicates that art education was of beneficial importance to society because it could advance the 'higher qualities' of welfare maximisation overall, expressing our human associations, the painful and the pleasurable human experiences of life that cohere with our own thoughts. However portrayed, a novel with pain expressed in it, when discussed in a class situation with facility, exactness and relevence, is hardly something that should escape anyone's notice, be unexamined and not personally weighed. In association, the sympathy and conformity that to some extent reveal turns of thought requisite for student contemplation and improvement helps places oneself 'in' its point of view. By means of the art itself, the art work speaks to us informatively, appealing to our imagination and understanding, in ways that can enlarge our mental powers and happy existence. In this manner, student art production can create vivid conceptions that can be imaginatively perceived in different ways as the incidents of life essential to furthering welfare maximisation overall.

For example, art teachers look at or hear the student's art work and find it to be impressive. I have been indicating how this is possible but further elucidation is needed. If the art produced by the student is impressive this is not simply because the student has carried out their exercise with the measurements or any other requirements that the teaching task has stipulated. For example, if the teacher of art tells the student that they are to write a 'short story describing their Christmas holiday with a beginning, middle and an end to it' and left it at that, the short stories handed in as a result of this exercise from the students probably would not be that impressive at all. Welfare maximization overall in this exercise has fallen by the wayside. To get it back on track we would be looking for those inputs from the teacher that excite student interest in the idea of the exercise. Student's capabilities naturally affect their results, but how well the exercise was explained to them also correspondingly affects student's achievements. Hence, to stimulate the class, the students' understanding is in proportion to their being in the world and what they are capable of grasping and achieving are clearly teaching issues. Furthermore, having set this task we are going to have to know, as teachers, what such a task has got to do with common human happiness. This is an important realisation, one of many realisations that the teacher of art is familiar with as it connects to welfare maximization overall. For one of the essential conditions of any society is the experiences we share arising from

5

our common human happiness that affects in lots of different ways the practice of living a good life, of resolutions, disagreements and connections expressing what is colourful, funny, delightful, beautiful, sad, frustrating, relevant and exciting containing analogously "the states of mind produced by moral judgements" (Kant, 1928, p. 225).

We want the students to express the superior qualities of their aesthetic insight in connection to what belongs to the learning exercise. So in setting the theme for a short essay entitled 'Christmas Holiday' it is necessary to introduce into this exercise, the forms of life that concern the kinds of ordinary incidents, observations and reflections involving the adopted, conventional, written language refinement that will aid the students' self-identification of the good, the bad, the memorable and the routine in relation to their Christmas holiday. The kind of literature reading that the students are familiar with together with their previous submitted essays of a literary nature and showing some good, past student examples of this exercise will clearly help current student achievement in this matter. What these students are to describe imaginatively, in simple elevated ways as part of their education are the scenes, incidents, presents, people, games, weather, places, sport events, expectations, surprises, enjoyments, reflections and concerns, relating to their Christmas holidays, that are of a shared, common, social interest. The life accounts that the students then express become beneficial as these life accounts are tempered by thoughts and feelings comprising of their understanding owing to their experience, interest and capability for retaining and improving on reflection students' happiness in life. These literary essays in a firm social-moral manner reveal how an art education can enable the students to become more aware of themselves, their personal deliberations and inclinations, paying regard to others, their circumstances and the world around them in interconnected, affective ways. In introducing this task, the student de-briefing thoughts after the event, teacher class feedback and in individual written comments, the teacher can highlight and reinforce to the students the value of the exercise where recognition of how one felt or did not feel, what one did or did not do, are important learner-like comprehensions and comparisons of character, temperament, behavior, objection, desire and delight. When making such conceptions involving further adjustments and reflections, that over time increases the power of certain acknowledged critical judgements and imagination acting in accordance with such exercise ends, the students become more mindful of themselves, their distinctions and their environment.

A student's art work may be judged inaccurate when their work is presented for assessment purposes due to the fact that they did not include the correct measurements or any other requirement that the task demanded. This is not strictly an aesthetic matter until a student can make something and do something with the measurements in an aesthetic fashion. Knowing that the measurements of a glass beaker are one hundred and fifty millimetres in height by eighty millimetres in diameter only becomes an aesthetic issue when we use the measurements in an applied, imaginative, artistic manner. The measurements here do not state the actual glass properties for the beaker, the thickness, heaviness and lightness of it, its shape, texture, decoration, colour or design. Students are expected to particularise and recognise in individual, art, learner-like ways, utilising the powers of their practical and creative thinking, what properties, ideas and qualities will produce the correct attributable effect in appearance of how aptly things should look, move, express or sound like, of how an appearance, for example, with such-and-such a look or sound appears frightening, for example.

The student in an art lesson is empowered to make decisions of their own because they have been encouraged by the teacher to think of art qualities, ideas and properties in certain conceptual-perceptual ways that will enable them to grasp the grounds springing from themselves that affects their own progress in their art activity connected to the general identity that the art task has defined. Human happiness, being influenced by superior qualities, is also related to the student being able to enlarge their feelings, actions, gestures and thoughts in respect to reasons and claims supporting their art. For the student that wants to exert more precisely in the displayed performance or in a poem, for example, a moral sentiment-benefit that has deliberately come from the envisaged way the art has been conceived and created, an art of this kind must have the formal peculiarities representative of the general state of the moral sentiment-benefit that the art has cultivated. As Berys Gaut (2007) mentions in his book *Art, Emotion and Ethics*, a sensitively recorded moral incident in a play can partly constitute the beauty of the art work. Beauty is synonymous with human happiness.

An art production "can express and develop our understanding of who we are and of what matters to us—a thought that Hegel developed in his idea of art as the articulation of a culture's self-understanding" (Gaut, 2007, p. 6). Gaut's account of art certainly signifies the common good since we see the value of art at times when it explores moral issues that are part of a larger share of public moral value in life. It expresses human happiness from the ordinary, rare and the particular in a common conveyed quality of an art tackling such issues in satisfying moving ways, which shows socially good and bad motives and actions, argues Martha Nussbaum (1996) in *The Fragility of Goodness*.

For a utilitarian like Mill, what is the right or wrong thing to do, in general, involves perceptions in the concrete (Mill, 2007, p. 2) that strengthen our values in moral, intellectual, aesthetic and social living. What is right and what is wrong for a student to do in an art class is a germane educational issue. To throw more light on the notions of right and wrong actions that can affect teaching judgements, Mill further suggests that right actions proportionately tend to promote human happiness and wrong actions proportionately tend to promote pain, frustration or suffering. Hence, while actions, rules and consequences matter in our lives, they only matter in a utilitarian fashion if they promote human happiness with everyone in mind overall. Educationally what this means is that in thinking about the actions that the student might take in various situations corresponding to art related practices, they become guided by teacher-public concerns which affect their actions. Because the teacher of art is consistent in the way they handle art teaching issues and in the way they discuss issues of art with their students that correspond to the right kinds of actions and the contingent understanding, it enables the students to make progress and experience more common human happiness.

Why there can be justifiable enjoyment when what is produced by a student of art who decides to express a scene of pain or suffering in a painterly representative manner, whose image in its estimated magnitude and depth can correspondingly rectify the failure or defeat its pain or the suffering shown, is because as Aristotle mentions, the art is seen as redeeming due to the art's portrayed performance proving to be cathartic, of what we have noticed to be of the sharpest aesthetic perception-cognition. I believe, for reasons that I have begun to state, that there is not enough debate explaining why art educational experiences are vital for a proper understanding of our world.

A corollary of Mill's concept of human happiness that Roger Crisp explains is how: "Utilitarianism says not only that one should perform those actions that produce the most happiness, but that one's very character should also be directed to the same end. In the later essay on Bentham, Mill expands on this notion. Mill sees morality as concerned not only with the regulation of actions, but with the self-education of the sentiments. This is so not merely because the student's character affects the action-thought activity of the art creation, which in turn affects the level of happiness overall, though of course this matters. Rather, self-education is important in coming to understand the nature of happiness itself, and is itself a constituent of happiness" (Crisp, 1997, p. 11–12). A student can learn how 'a house has character' and how a novel's qualities can describe within it a person's personality reflecting who they are, for their smiles, wit, cheer, cheekiness, excitement, kindness, deviousness or dishonesty so portrayed in the novel, denotes a judgement we make of the character of them. Crisp is aware that Mill's notion of self-education of the sentiments can seem to imply that an oligarch, a corrupt or selfish egoist can benefit from their own right actions as they self-conceive them. Noting this dilemma, Mill states that right actions "always act from the inducement of promoting the general interests in society" (Mill, 2007, p. 15). The validity of the students' art judgements and that of the teachers' art judgements in education conjointly involve welfare maximisation concerns. A curriculum of art in a utilitarian fashion, would know consequentially what an art can maximize in welfare flourishing ways with limits and opportunities leveling, increasing and proving ordinarily imposed standards that the art's curriculum human associations in a consensual, collective, social manner can generate.

Right actions involve the interests of everyone agreeing to the common acts and obligations of the art curriculum so that "someone can act" accordingly (Williams, 1997, p. 46). We cannot be teaching art properly if only a few of the students in the class have the capabilities to act correctly. If only ten percent of the art class students are meeting the academic benchmark standards, something is wrong. Bearing in mind, in addition, that Mill remarks that the quality of art is an essential factor that facilitates welfare maximisation overall in society. Thus, if the students are not expressing through experience how art production adds meaning to society, the students' ability to act appropriately with feeling, imagination and understanding in the wider sphere of life, of things common which can affect numbness, blankness, dimness, vagueness, gentleness, uncompanionship, expressionist, noblest and loveliness actions of life, for example, will the student experience more frustration, helplessness, strangeness, weakness, darkness, isolation, pain and suffering?

Simon Blackburn remarks in relation to Utilitarianism: "just as a lot of crimes are committed in the name of liberty, so they can be committed in the name of the common happiness" (Blackburn, 2001, p. 89). So certainly art education should not fall head-over-heels into an art-for-arts sake regime of art activity. Just as it should not fall head-over-heels for a social and ethical regime of art, since no single factor explains fully the diverse productions of art that moves us freely or which we escape to and yet we need a society that regularly and standardily shows higher cooperation, rationality, moral values, human sympathetic feeling and aesthetic qualities.

How to estimate whether art educational welfare maximisation overall is successful, as I have been attempting to explain, is in proportion to the quality of art that the art curriculum standards and subject-matter content range has defined, the conjoined quality of the teaching pedagogy, the conjoined quality of the student's experiences and the conjoined quality of the student's produced art work, as factors together demonstrating such entailment. These factors together, under different arrangements, conditions, situations and circumstances contribute to the educational relevance of art in society. But for art education to demonstrate that welfare maximisation overall is being fully realised art education has to show, through examples of student work, the revealing student learner-like capacities attaining and enlarging the properties and characteristics of the 'higher pleasures' of human happiness.

Art in education has to know the quality of the art that is being taught, produced and learnt and "the most effective means for the inculcation" (Mill, 2007, p. 8) of the quality-experience of art in education. The purpose of any art exercise and the resulting, relevant art outcomes that make us sensible to it affect the right quality of teaching in art relating to the art exercise and the right student understanding-capacity and the right extent of the quality of the learning experience that the teaching is aiming to achieve. This does not mean that what is right about the X quality factor that the teaching is aiming for is numerical or formulaic, but rather that some reasons, concepts, imagination, properties and qualitites, more than others, are stimulating the whole class and appealing to a shared standard about the art exercise requirements. Individual teaching input relating to different student ability levels and different student interests and their approaches furthers the success of the art exercise.

Bernard Williams states that morally "I may be under the obligation through no choice of mine...once I am under the obligation, there is no escaping it, and the fact that a given agent would prefer not to be in this system or bound to its rules will not excuse him or her" (Williams, 1997, p. 48). Clearly, children are obliged by law to go to school, which for good paternalistic reasons override the child's choice in this instance: choosing whether to be educated or not to be educated is not a choice for the child to make. Everyone agrees that education is good for children and there is much proof that this benefits their human happiness. However, Mill would further say that human happiness is only beneficial when we are able "to think more broadly about the special human capacities that contribute to happiness" (Noddings, 2005, p. 19).

Mill maintained that the quality of life for everyone should reconcile proportionately, with prudence, the happiness of others as well as that of our own happiness and the pursuit of it involving our happiness together in life communally to affect how welfare maximisation overall is being exercised and distributed, promoting the possibility of the general good in everyone and the good of the whole community (Mill, 2007, p. 15). Welfare maximisation overall was the best proof of a system that in proportion would enable human happiness to be realised potentially by all.

There are several further important adjustments that Mill makes to his notion of welfare maximisation overall, that I will go on to explore because it has to do with the idea of 'quality' that can bring home to us further an art's educational relevance in the teaching of art. Before I do, even with these adjustments to his notion of human happiness, Kant produces a major objection to the notion of utility that also has a bearing on art teaching and student learning about art.

I have expressed the common enough idea that art activity must have its imaginative freedom, a caprice which Hegel suggested in his *Aesthetics* is lacking in the real world of practicalities. Part of Kant's view is similar to this, that art creation is "incapable of resting on the representation [of] utility" (Kant, 1928, §. 15). Art is not *techne* but it has *techne* in it. Utility has a preconceived definite end, Kant declares, of what the art production is meant to be in the concrete. It has a universal rule, he thinks, determining what art should look like or be performed as. Kant argues, convincingly, that this is what will cramp the mind of art production and experience and contain it, stifling the need to enlarge the mental habits of art experience and understanding. I must feel the pleasure immediately in the art object, argues Kant, which means correctly that I cannot be talked into it "by any grounds of proof" (Kant, 1928, §. 34). But Kant, like Hume, believed that the best form of art production is always a personal, conjoined, higher, inner feeling and thought experience producing a near resemblance of the outward manifestation of the art reflecting the student's sensibility relative to a subjective free conformity of understanding consisting of associated moral, intellectual, common pleasures and common human sympathies of life. The conceptual nature of this construct indicates a major difference between the way we teach art and the way we teach science. Yet, there is something odd about "I must feel the pleasure" in the art object if this is no more than a lethargic indolence incapable of recognising in variety why Isabel Rorick's and Robert Davidson's Haida hat object of 2003, Jackson Pollock's 1948 *Summertime No.9a*, Picasso's 1937 *Guernica*, Edgar Dega's 1865 *A women with Chrysanthemums* and Jan Vermeer's 1665 *The Artist in the Studio*, for example, are important works of art that for different reasons any delight that we might take from such art works must be attributed in part to their appearances and intentions. This is why, Kant argued, at the very beginning of *The Critique of Judgement* that I must not only feel the pleasure of the art object I must also understand it "with a view to cognition by means of the imagination" while considering the art work. In addition, hasn't art activity always used rules of one kind or another for determining a certain underlying principle of an art? A teacher of art would not object, for example, to different Aboriginal traditions, or Egyptian, Byzantine, Greek, Renaissance, Romantic, Impressionistic, Surrealist and Modernist conventions, whose philosophies involve facts, concepts, theories, ideas, criticisms and rules of an art.

A work of art "pleases freely on its own account" (Kant, 1928, §. 16). Is this to be regarded as an important human happiness principle? A utilitarian like Mill could not object to this and as he explores in his *Autobiography* (Mill, 2008, p. 74–100), it was such thinking that enabled him to overcome his mental depression. Much later in *The Critique of Judgement,* Kant says that an art's work possesses a feeling connected to its quality that "adapts itself to our mode of taking it in" (Kant, 1928, §. 32). Either we find the art pleasurable or displeasurable, the effect of both conditions are founded on a subjective judgement of the shared value of the art. However, if "taste lays claim simply to autonomy" (Kant, 1928, §. 32) this can only be because we share similar thoughts about the art, where taste, for Kant, is referring to the quality of the art, that in a different but similar sense, Mill also expands upon discursively in a number of his works. Mill agrees that the imagination is essential to art activity, to human experience, concurring with Hegel that art activity and experience is also "one of the main ways in which human beings plumbs the depth of the world" revealing and actualizing him or herself, "reflected off the world as off a mirror" (Hegel, 1993, pp. xviii–xix). Art activity is not mere imitation and nor is it just mimetic activity as though these were the only aims of an art, but it is also a free productive force that confronts us with the common opinion that the task and aim of art is to bring home to us our sense, our feeling, and our inspiration everything which has a place in the human spirit. That familiar saying *'nihil humani a me alienum puto'* [I count nothing human indifferent to me], art is supposed to make real in us" (Hegel, 1988, p. 46). How much of this paragraph alone is suggestive of how the quality of art cultivates the quality of life? It is worth discussing educationally that art is a mirror, that art is not a mirror, and that what is made real to us is the qualities that the art really does possess, as John Hyman (2006) discusses in *The Objective Eye* together with the arts ideas and concepts and what we deeply feel is moving about art as Iris Murdoch (1993) discusses in *Metaphysics as a Guide to Morals* and Martha Nussbaum (1986) discusses in *the Fragility of Goodness.*

If our understanding of the quality of an art work contains what we feel is representative of our common human spirit and intelligence related to the appropriate pathos of the art and its refinement, a respect for moral ideals and moral feelings that Kant (1928) mentions in *The Critique of Judgment,* does art in education then have a wholesome notion, a certain understanding of life's harmony, an infused serious reverence in the play of our common continuous life judgements that stand out about the world? Mill certainly thought so.

11

How is a teacher of art expected to teach art with a class full of children with easels, a dark room, potters wheels, sewing machines, a stage and with a group of fourteen year old students and their violins, who are confronted for the first time with learning to play Johann Pachelbel's *Canon*? What will the students detect from the art teacher? What qualities, concepts and ideas in a teaching situation will students perceive from the teacher that will enable them to produce the kind of consequences that shows to them, that they are advancing, adjusting and being inspired by their teaching instruction?

In order to develop the quality expected in an art exercise, Dewey maintains that "if our view of the world consisted of a succession of momentary glimpses, it would be no view of the world nor anything in it. If the roar and the rushing stream of Niagara were limited to an instantaneous noise and peep, there would not be perceived the sound or sight of any object, much less of the particular object called Niagara Falls. It would not be grasped even as a noise. Nor would mere isolation continuation of the external noise beating on the ear effect anything except increased confusion. Nothing is perceived except when different senses work in relation with one another" (Dewey, 1980, p. 175). There is a clear sense in this that the student must go back to the art and revisit it, that the creation of art at times is not a quick observation or a quickly conceived thought. "The idea of attention or contemplation, of looking carefully at something and holding it…is moral training as well as preparation for a pleasurable life" (Murdoch, 1993, p. 3). From the art teacher in the class comes clarity and capability, the learner-like issues that will have an essential bearing on the art that they want the students to complete and that will involve the amount of information the students will need in order to achieve a more precise discrimination and conceiving by means of the connections, relations, contrasts and apprehensions adapted to the art task of a deeper study, performance and elevation.

Mill, like Kant, Hegel, Nietzsche and Heidegger, recognised that art production "cuts fresh channels for thought, but it does not fill up such as it finds ready-made, but it traces, on the contrary, more deeply, broadly, and distinctively, those into which the current has spontaneously flowed" (Mill, 1897, p. 202). So if the art is the students' construction, their self-consciousness, of their own desires and interest and of their own impulse and excitement, which is what Kant and Hegel imply art activity and experience involves, Mill can still agree with them but further maintains that quality in art matters to accomplish a higher standard of critical judgement, directing awareness and achievement in art education that is its substantial end.

THE QUALITY OF ART

...the composer may draw on a huge repertory of available styles—old and new, sacred and secular—and may combine them at will. This freedom lies at the heart of extraordinary expressive power of the Vespers.

(Keyte & Parrott, 1984, p. 1)

Having introduced the idea of quality in art education it is time to investigate it further relating it more to a teaching context. The idea of quality in art is firmly connected to the idea of autonomy in art but the autonomy of art is not the whole cause that we need to be acquainted with as teachers in respect to the conditions concerning the quality of art that is produced in learner-like art educational ways. One of the most important aspects of utilitarianism which affects the teaching of art and learning quality is why we should "raise the floor of benefits as high as possible for our society...is to everyone's benefit even if they benefit some more than others" (Slote, 1998, p. 99). How might the quality of art education benefit some students more than others may depend on the students' interest, motivation, labor, strength of thought, imagination and prior experiences, for example. Interconnectedly, it will also depend on the students individually converting and transforming, for themselves, the teaching stimulation that has attempted to cause the relevant development of understanding and ideas so the students can act in conformity in a general way taking account of the actions, representations and concepts that will affect their performance and production.

We need to go back to Mill in order to reconsider how he perceives social, ethical, intellectual and aesthetic benefit in utilitarian ways. "The most effective means for the inculcation" of an estimated practice of art is "when we engage in a pursuit with a clear and precise conception of what we are pursuing as the first thing we need, instead of the last we are looking forward to" (Mill, 2007, p. 2). One of the first things I believe we need to pay more attention to is the social learner-like experiences of art in education. There is pedagogy to consider that involves, with the student in mind, how to deliver a quality learning environment of art in education. There is the reality of time constraining factors that affect what can be reasonably taught in education with only X number of hours available to teach art in an academic year.

Having a clear, precise conception of the teaching we are going to deliver, is an effective way of inculcating the ideas, thoughts and practices that proportionately relate to the idea of quality that the teacher wants the students in an art class, studio, workshop or theatre to realise and experience. It is a plain fact that if a student is unable to focus on the issue at hand in an art lesson, they cannot be learning very much, if anything at all. However, the conversation we have with students begins with motivational issues that students can relate to, with art pictures and student's paintings on walls, students being taken to classical music concerts, students being taken to a major theatre, ballet or modern dance performances, students playing their recorders in class and "look, listen, isn't that pretty, isn't that nice"? (Murdoch, 1993, p. 3).

Mill maintains that the principle we should use in deciding what kind of art activity to teach students involves the idea of welfare maximisation overall that in turn is conjoined to the 'great happiness principle'. Since utilitarianism was a response to human happiness in life, Mill argued that our character, conduct and actions of the quality of our human happiness represented a moral standard of life, and at a system, character, conduct and action level, welfare in society had to consist of sharing more equally life's "greatest happiness principle" (Mill, 2007, p. 3); the influence of utility. As previously pointed out, some students may benefit from welfare maximisation overall more than others. Some students will make more of their opportunities than others. But in an educational manner a curriculum of art and the teaching of art have to be delivered in an equal proportionate way to the entire student class. All students are treated equally in ethical ways. Thus, teaching the whole student group with attention given equally to each student in the class knowing their capabilities and concerns so that every student can make progress in the art lesson, experience the relevance and intensity of the art activity and the superior qualities of art would be one example of welfare maximization overall in art education enabling human happiness.

If we are considering what are the right actions to adopt this philosophy may start with; what does a teacher of art have to know when teaching music, dance, acting, literature and poetry, design, crafts, film, architecture, photography and fine art, for example, at a particular level? A teacher of art would have to know about the psychological and sociological contemporary currents that are related to learning issues. Teachers have to know about the ethics of teaching. They would have to know a little about the history of education and important pedagogical reformers. They would have to know about different pedagogical approaches. They would have to know about the pleasures and the beauty of an educational life. They would have to know about the students' capabilities, their personalities and their sense of themselves. There is an educational love that the teacher must have for all their students. They would have to know something about the aims and purpose of education, and they would equally have to know about the instrumental, methodological, instructional and organisational aspects of a school, college and university curriculum of art, involving the attainment standards in teaching and learning appropriate to these institutions. Teachers need regularly to draw upon and share their teaching experiences amongst their colleagues in different focus-point team meetings in order to reach on-going consensus about changes that affect the teaching of art. These factors represent some of the scholarship, professionalism and accountability measures of an education system. So all things considered, on the face of it, art education looks nicely balanced when embracing these factors and more besides, since they form part of the wealth and cognisance attributed to good teaching in art. But focus-point team meetings in themselves may tell us nothing in particular about the quality of art in education until the quality of art is part of such an agenda. It is art that the art teacher is teaching. Various teaching practices of art in education can struggle to get a proper hearing and produce a convincing argument that consist in an agreement. Obviously there are many teaching aspects in art education that interrelate along different lines. There is a curriculum of art that is sequentially and developmentally designed to be accepted by everybody teaching art and there are aspects in art education that profitably go their own separate ways to explore different outlooks and produce different works of art by students in a class, conservatory, studio or workshop environment.

Whatever the different teaching approaches that an art curriculum in its breadth and depth requires, all art teaching abides and concurs with what the maximum probable benefits from the curriculum range of devised student activities overall are. Having curriculum knowledge and lesson planning understanding in art is clearly beneficial. An arts curriculum content plays a substantive role determining what actions and consequences are good, holding common judgements and commitments about art that an art teacher knows substantially affects the successful production of art in education in ways designed to strengthen, harness, improve and stretch the student's capabilities of art comprehension and production. The exercises of an art curriculum connect strongly to prior student experiences, but not always necessarily so, since new experiences may be very different from previous experiences, so that different outlooks-practices have to be learnt anew.

A curriculum of art takes as a pedagogical given the students' personal perceptions, thoughts, actions and articulations, their responses, experiences and awareness in this or that way in accordance to the required art exercise. A curriculum plan cannot begin to appreciate that all students are different and that they have different character traits. Without pedagogy, art examples, art experiences in the concrete, discussions and training in art, the curriculum of art as presented to the inexperienced student, will leave them empty of the correct habits they will need to form in order to advance the best possible results that relate to the intentions of the art task in hand. The students may know what the lesson intentions require but still have no idea how to realise precisely its requirements and direct their actions and thinking efficiently, particularly and productively.

Art curricula acknowledge that it is the students' personal experiences and their intellectual capabilities that have to be harnessed for the sake of the art task. The sensible habits of actions, ideas, cooperation, and reflection contain the various teaching and learning instances that affect progress in the art activity. A curriculum states the art's external requirements, but remains quiet about how to precisely teach the art that its requirements demand. How to explore, play and think in certain ways; how to appreciate 'this', take account of 'this', identfy what 'this' entails and how to imagine 'this', the art teaching task postulates in ways that have to be adequate to students' understanding. This indicates further how important pedagogy is in education. The students' ideas, actions and thoughts are left to the art teacher to approach in ways which support the students' development in their art exercise. No curriculum of art states the conditions that will individually, particularly and singularly supply the sensuous imagery and cognition of the object-performance of the right sort of constructed movements, material techniques, actions, remarks and gestures for the student to observe, experience and reflect upon in a class. Adequate examples with explanations may be given to act as models that stir student thinking and appreciation but they are no substitute for the creative self-conscious mind fancying, struggling upwards and developing, the productive ideas of the student whose object emerges on its own account but not independent from the examples given. The examples given can act as the catalyst that induces the required kind of creative activity obtained through guidance that impresses the relevance of the examples and in connection the student adapted sympathetic cultivation of the art example that widens and deepens their understanding. Each student in a class is encouraged to discover things for themselves and to imaginatively project images, actions and thoughts in material and performance ways.

Art teachers recognise that the students' own views of an art task affect how the teachers teach art. An art teacher knows what their students are generally thinking about because they have a continuous on-going dialogue with them about their art work. They will know what their students already know about art due to their past experiences and previous tasks. The art teacher knows what capabilities each student possesses through the accomplished performances and exercises they have completed as the prime evidence of their current achievement. They also know what they want to achieve in a class because they have discussed with the students what they intend to do and they know how the students are going to accomplish their end in view by what they have identified, explained, understood, shown in appearance and by the steps they are going to take in order to facilitate the performance, ideas and interpretations that the art task requires. They will know how the student is going to play this piece of music on the piano because they have agreed with them their approach, their reading of the music and because of their past performance of it. The art teacher knows what their students are actually contemplating as they reflect, produce and perform due to the actions that they take and due to changes in the art work that are more discriminately or less discriminately of what is required. The teacher will know if the students have understood what is required of them by asking questions of them, by addressing their questions, through a sequence of learner-like events that may pause in the middle to assess student understanding that then subsequently requires some further explanation from teacher enabling the student to become more familiar, for example, of some notable relevant quality, concept, action and idea. Equally, the teacher will moderate students' work throughout the entire lesson for the relevant signs of student progress and understanding in order to appropriately correct, indicate, direct, encourage and discuss student learner-like problem issues as they arise. All this requires an atmosphere, as Parsons and Blocker (1993) mention in *Aesthetics and Education*, of support, articulation, elaboration, reflection, acceptance and facilitation.

The student experiences in an art lesson contains important learner-like situations for the art teacher as well as obviously for the student. The art teacher understands an art curriculum in terms of the aims and outcomes of what its construct concerns, its rational justification and the merits of it stimulating the kind of evidence that are the targets-outcomes for a task. Hence, art teachers will know the range of experiences, ideas, performances and properties of the art activity that they know in reliable and correct ways, of the standard contributions from them that will typify students' realisations of how certain processes, characteristics, performances and ideas for the art activity under given circumstances follows, that has resulted in the expected and the unexpected surprising results of the art production that has satisfied the various demands of the task.

It is also to be noted that the art teacher discusses the required and particular kind of receptivity that the task's intentions demand from the student. Yet the levity of this occurs when the student becomes more aware and adjusts to the art teaching perspective that is artistically encouraging how different inferences, tones, interpretations and intonations can be made in justifiable ways by the student. Setting the scene that prudently becomes restricted due to prior experiences, capabilities and the art work's objectives are standard aspects of what an art teacher does. Such attentiveness by the teacher of art advances, in an underlying way, the measure and scale of the students' self-determining learner-like actions, their recall and focusing powers bringing into play the students' estimated common understanding of a certain practice of art that in an enhanced and enabling manner the art teacher has directed. Students derive a lot of enjoyment from what they are able to achieve, which is an important aspect of pedagogy.

I have been partly explaining the general kind of right actions and their nuances that a teacher of art recommends to their students in a class. Mill thought of right actions as being in proportion to the common good and characteristic of welfare maximisation overall. Importantly, whatever the right actions are, they enable students to acquire the higher qualities for realising, entertaining, promoting and increasing human happiness conducive to the common good. High qualities are the discernible results of students deploying their intellectual, aesthetic, moral, social and practical thinking. If right actions increase human happiness, wrong actions, Mill believed, are the powers that negate the higher qualities. Wrong actions tend to lead to human problems and difficulties whereas the higher qualities "increase our sum total of happiness" (Mill, 2007, p. 14).

No student deliberately sets out to answer anything wrongly nor deliberately tries to under achieve. What may be wrong with the student art work is conversely in proportion to the right action, yet what may be wrong with their art work is also an opportunity to improve their art work. Wrong thoughts can become sensible thoughts for getting things right by grasping what was wrong with the art performance. Wrong thoughts in such instances serve a purpose for getting things right in the art work. It may well be because of the mistakes that the student has produced in their art work that, on reflection, makes them realise more appreciatively the idea, performance or the concept and the associated experiences of them, reaffirming, increasing and fostering more of their interest which previously the student had taken for granted. It is worth noting that singing in the wrong key, not putting enough colour contrast in the painting and being unable to properly do a *pas de ciseaux* are the type of challenges that may be good for the student, stiffening their resolve, reducing worry and anxiety when problems occur. Equally, an unobserved, sluggish, ill-adapted, scrappy, frantic, over-indulged, crude and uncontrolled few swipes of the paint brush, not knowing when to stop with chisel marks on the scultural piece the student is working on or adding a few further written lines of a poem may erase the correct expression one once had. Alternatively, a crudely played set of music notes, a dance movement performance, or a sketched scene in a play, for example, may be something that the student wants to retain because such incidents are beginning to indicate an alternative provocation of an idea that on reflection they are now imaginatively seeing the potential of its lively physical properties that once was anonymous to them. A mistake does not necessarily discredit a student's thinking or make them incapacitated, but rather can galvanize them out of their stupor, giving their consciousness the kick where it is needed that rekindles their satisfaction and their appetite for art.

Good sense is shown by the student when they can recognise that they have a problem with executing the art task and furthermore when they: 'can now see the error they have made'. The twist in the tail here is the inducement, the encouragement, the drawing upon past experiences and achievements, the willingness to revisit the problem, to learn from other students in the class, to do more work, and to recognise that problems are part-and-parcel aspects of learning; a problem recognised is an achievement in itself. When a student does not understand what the teacher of art has suggested to them, the teacher may have to resort to efforts that compare the student's thinking with their own thinking. How the student and the teacher are picturing things differently about the art concept or using their hands or their body language in such a way that each is expressing a different musical or acting capacity. The teacher of art has to respect differences of the student's attributed values about an art exercise and at the same time be aware that cultural differences are maybe causing the problem to exist (Wittgenstein, 1980, p. 83). Progress rather than perfection matters most in learning. Consequently, tackling an art task that requires production in it related to its problem, is good in itself, a reflection of the true character of a student's higher qualities in action. Mistakes, errors and problems with this or that in the art work can encourage self-belief, the ability to postulate further what needs to change in the art production. Mistakes bring out reasons and actions we simply have not meditated upon previously. Problems often relate to the particular circumstances and situations the student finds themselves in. What is wrong with the performance may be easily remedied when, for example, a teacher says 'play it like this'. But knowing we are performing the music wrongly may also take some time to remedy. It may require a great deal of practice to 'play it like this' and in playing it 'like this' what must the student grasp in order to play it 'like this'? The student's uncertainty about what to do to correct their problem is a teaching issue. Students may be aware of their mistakes but solving the problems they are experiencing may take some time to resolve. It may need to be broken up into chunks and stages in order to make their problems more manageable in ways that doing 'this' and doing 'that' show progress. A wrong action may occur because a student did not stop to reflect on their problem or the fact that they knew they had a problem but decided to ignore it rather than address it. This might result in another wrong action being taken or a repeat of the same problem, only this time it could be an even bigger problem than before. A wrong action might be the result of misreading what was required or because we were impatient, unfocused and disinterested. There are clearly many reasons why wrong actions result in problems and frustrations.

Mill thought that what makes an action right is how it sustains and extends our human sympathies, aesthetic experiences, intellectual, practical and moral existence. Right actions are able to bring forward not just one's own self-interest but many other reasons that have a real relation and bearing upon one's self-interest. Separating one's own self-interest as a world completely indifferent to other persons self-interest in order to maximize one's own happiness can become irresistible. But it was more natural, Mill thought, that human beings would want to share their happiness befitting of what a human life is. We are social creatures even when we are selfish (though we may deny it) because we want to be noticed, we want to feel self-important. We live in a social world where cooperation and friendship is the conventional norm. All teachers know how important cooperation and friendship is for student well-being. A further point about right actions is to some extent their habit forming importance. However, mistakes in a performance, a drawing, a garment or in writing a poem, for example, are what can prevent our human sympathies for the performance, drawing, garment or the written poem. If a student performs, draws, makes an object or writes a poem without expressing the higher qualities of the art, what is produced in this way more broadly reflects their own character, intellect and morality of life seen as indifferent to the common good, or perhaps poor teaching has provided insufficient guidance in these matters.

Thinking purely of oneself, Mill rejected for social and moral reasons because self-interest cannot represent proof of our understanding of happiness. Self-interest fails to take account of the majority of people's views concerning happiness in life. Why other people's views about happiness matter in the world and correspondingly should be part of the totality of one's own views about happiness that contributes to one's happiness, is Mill's ideal notion of human happiness overall. Social, democratic agreement, he maintained, was the best way to maximise happiness overall in life for everyone. Blackburn remarks that "utilitarianism started with the ambition of breaking down the separateness that gives a person no concern for us apart from me" (Blackburn, 2001, p. 93). It is not difficult to recognise that moral, social, intellectual and aesthetic beneficial experiences are the acts that can maximise happiness in human social welfare overall ways. Mill saw right actions were good for society if they strengthened our deeds and their consequences that focused on the advantages of welfare maximisation overall for the public common good in society of the 'great happiness principle'.

We cannot presuppose what quality judgment a teacher is going to make about a student's art work without them seeing the actual student's art work first. We also know that during the creation of the art and the accompanying developmental process of it, there are going to be learner-like aspects about the quality of the art that are proper to the conception of 'this' art practice, educating the student about how to achieve the higher standard of an art conspiringly transforming the art activity through a human context. The student is instructed by the teacher of art in situational, circumstantial and developmental ways to consider, reconcile and respond appropriately to what their physical movements on stage or thoughts, actions and feelings are reciprocally arousing, counteracting, contradicting, confirming and confronting in order to bring home the sense of the art that is required at any one moment shaping and forming the art the student is producing.

In all art teaching areas (discipline based or not) common and ordinary life teaching remarks to students in an art class might include in important, sophisticated, sometimes difficult and in simply put ways: the orange-yellowness of the painting, the charcoal drawing of your dandelion flower is light and airy, the contrast of a black bird with green pines and blue sky in the print, a saucer of milk for the cat in a poem, a boat at sea in a storm, tears shed for a departing friend in a story, darkness turning plants pale, a fine elastic thread for a garment, hay bales in the field, the sound of drifting sand in the wind, the waving undulating sound of tall grass, a river shining like silver and a game of chess. A student remarks to their teacher that 'this morning riding my bicycle to school I could feel the cold morning air on my face, I clicked my gears, bent down, gripped harder my handlebars and sped down Harley street as fast as I could...' and the teacher responds by suggesting why don't you now write a short story about your bicycle journey. In a drama class the teacher remarks that they want the student to 'act like you are a key about to open a door'. 'Having completed a number of different observational mixed-media, experimental, idea bascd, and decorative sketch drawing exercises over the past two weeks from the nuts and foliage on the drawing class tables, I now want the class to convert these drawings of the large collection of different nuts on the table that is still before you, continuing to use these objects as a reference, as objects to return to and investigate at will but with a different purpose today in mind. In the assignment notes I have handed out at the beginning of this work you will see that for the final two-weeks of this assignment I now want you to move your drawings on, with the familiarity and confidence you have acquired relating to the several different observational drawing exercises, experimentation and ideas we have covered involving how you wanted to express these nut drawings, for example, in appearance that have been formed according to your thoughts as estimates that appear as: ancient objects, dark, solid, strong, wild, golden, colourful, diminutive, playful, large, earthly, alive, wrinkled, edible, delicious, festive, rough and strange looking fruits. Your task now is to produce, over the next two weeks, an abstract repeated pattern design that has a clear relationship to your nut drawings but with a developed abstract repeated pattern design of them. Using the A2 watercolour paper provided I want you to fill up this whole sheet using any single or mixed media painterly materials'. So what has been the point of these exercises in proportion to the welfare maximization overall concerns? In all of the above mentioned exercises are the experiences and effects of events, incidents and situations related to everyday life and their enjoyments and satisfactions with conceptions and ideas exploring and distinguishing quality of life experiences, of difficult and complex judgments, where the different art activities here are seeking to actualize and advance the students' cognitions, perceptions and imagination in a social communicative manner.

When experiences, thoughts and perceptions are advancing the students' art production, certain aspects and features are produced in a concrete material way that enable further imaginative feeling responses to advance and actualise more substantially the appearance-performance that is proper to the art task. These aspects unite, strengthen, and bring out the increased embodied appearance of the image and performance that more vividly and in conformity expresses the singular, individual and particular higher quality of the art on display. This is how art education in the teaching of art in relation to any practice of art generally tenders to the learner-like forces, concerns and conditions of an art that affects how the art student in relation to their capacities, creates excellence in the art in an appearance of perceived-cognitive-feeling communication. The students' capabilities at the level one is teaching art, are judged against the art task intentions-objectives-outcomes that subsequently affirms how excellence in teaching art will correspondingly assess the students' art work.

When we think of the quality that an art possesses, we invariably consider how traditional practices of art and the movements and genera of an art and the institutionalisation of art past and present have created particular standards, classes, notions, types, degrees and grades that have determined the excellences of different art activities. Within particular works of student art, we consider the quality of the art related to a teacher assessment estimate. This could involve the manner, skill, method, imagination, character, insight, rhythm, subject-matter and idea representative of some of the commonest and cherished feelings as performed, read, made and seen by the student. In doing so, we would be thinking particularly of the art qualities that have engaged the students' perceptions and cognition, noting how perhaps the tonal quality in the painting gives the student work an antique feel to the painting, a stiffness that suits the subject-matter in an unusual way, conjuring up, through properties of the art, an image of Roman inspired representation without the painting ever being so and without the student knowing this necessarily. The teacher of art makes a connection that the student is not aware of and need not have to be aware of. They may remark that 'I really did like the way you played this musical piece, it was excellent', or 'I don't think this colour is right', to then go on to explain why in both circumstances these judgements have been made. By using examples: 'play this', 'sing this like this', 'see this', 'write it with this kind of sentiment', 'think of this', an indication of how something should be done, realised or considered is being suggested that may need further illumination if the student does not recognise how to 'sing like this'.

An art lesson in a high school exploring further different qualities of an art might for instance use a visual display on a wall or a lecture with visual images to examine the differences and similarities in: squares, cubes, triangles, oblongs, ellipses in two-dimensional and three-dimensional orthographic ways, a Maori woodcarving, a farm house in Chad, the decoration of a Kassena house in Songo (Upper Volta), the Süleymaniye Mosque in Istanbul, a wooden bowl by David Pye, a blacksmith's tongs, a screen by Sakai Hōitsu, Seagram's skyscraper building by Mies van der Rohe in New York, Zaha Hadid's Hong Kong Innovation Tower, and Frank Gehry's EMP Seattle museum, for example.

In an art class, the art teacher decides to discuss having pre-planned it, why sketch productions relating to scenes, drawings, physical movements, models and samples, for example, have a quality to them that is equal or unequal to, or better than that of a finished piece of art work. The art teacher is introducing this concept because the students' understanding of the sophisticated process of art often begins at times with a sketch. As a notebook-sketchbook with a sequence of drawings in it, around a theme or an idea that is being investigated, the notebook-sketchbook also includes free-flowing unplanned drawings and notes. The notebook entries represent an understanding of the student creative thinking documenting their idea developments through the notebook-sketches which do not always follow a pattern. Serial and sequential images can be interrupted by changes in direction in the notebook-sketchbook. By drawing attention to sketches rather than the finished art work, a different activity is invoked. Drawings can be much looser, dynamic, fact finding, wide-ranging and inventive. The drawings can appear as though they are bouncing off one another in the notebook-sketchbook, constructing and deconstructing in explorative, creative, experimental, problem solving ways. Through various kinds of corrections, a clearer and more decisive picture of things tends to emerge.

In a student notebook-sketchbook, the art teacher sees scattered through it spontaneously captured figures and objects, incidents of daily life and responses to the environment or ideas that appear to have been immediately and reflectively produced. Many preparatory studies by the student have been made and the process itself is an inquiry attempting to document what appears as the student is thinking it, seeing it and altering the drawings in unexpected and magical ways. Evolving ideas are shown and changes are made to them: a leaf, a twig bent, a white flower, a hollow of a tree, a basket, a character's manner, a textile drawing finding its way, an object just beginning to be realised with further separate drawing, cataloguing details and much reworking shown with a variety of mixed-media applied. Each sketch might possess a reverence for the past or the present, a wild, swelling, controlled, chirpy, tumbling, faint, curling, pear-shaped, frosty and entertaining in their recognition of that which is an expression of an art's higher quality, the cultivation of enjoyment. What catches the teacher's eye is a leaf, a set of twig drawings, some plants, trees and rock drawings and in this instance they show and discuss with the students some of the drawings and sketches of Leonardo Da Vinci, Albrecht Dürer, Henri Matisse, Henry Moore, Robert Motherwell, Georgia O'Keeffe, Helen Frankenthaler, Freda Hansen, Otto Wagner, Otto Eckmann, Van Gogh, John Piper, Paul Cézanne and Monet. In this learner-like process, the emphasis is not on polished, finished work but on what the notebook-sketch qualities reveal. To the whole class the art teacher reads out and hands out a quote by André Malraux with three attached drawings to their handout: one from Rubens, Velázquez and Delacroix and in their usual manner starts a discussion with the students.

"The sketch which the greatest painters had marked out for preservation—Rubens, for instance, and Velázquez (in the case of his Gardens)—do not strike us as unfinished pictures, but as self-sufficient expressions which would lose much of their vigor, perhaps all, were they constrained to be representational. Though Delacroix declared the finished picture superior to the sketch, it was no accident that he preserved so many of his sketches; indeed their quality as works of art is equal to that of his best pictures" (Malraux, 1978, p. 110).

For a drama teacher to tell a student that they performed exceptionally well on stage in their role as Hamlet in Shakespeare's namesake play, is a judgement of quality implying that the student actor understood how the teacher wanted them to perform this role. When mentioning that a student's performance was good, we are recognising why it was relevant, triumphant, splendid and enjoyable. To enrich, enhance and refine a sketch that currently has a loose end to the music by adding more colour, more toughness to it, a crackling set of musical notes, a different metaphor that needs to be imagined or a soft touch winding down, are steps that might have to be thought about. To continue to rework a set of drawings, models, photographs, pages of a story and to reconstruct, refashion and rethink what the quality of an object or fashion garment should be is the path that the art activity in education takes by pedagogically refining the modes of intelligence that are right for the student's particular and singular art production, by being carefully conscious of the higher common pleasures of art.

AESTHETIC AND NON-AESTHETIC
TEACHING JUDGEMENTS

*In no other area of dictation is it so important to start with simple examples
and build slowly and progressively toward greater length and complication.*

(Rogers, 1984, 123)

Aesthetic and non-aesthetic qualities, properties, concepts, features and actions are some of the customary ways a student is taught art. For an example of a non-aesthetic quality that is referring to an art work's appearance, we might add an adverb to our comment like: 'the student lightly shaded in the object'. Hence, the object was not just shaded, it was lightly shaded, and that is telling us a little bit more about the object. As negligible and as relevant as this comment could be on occasion, something has been said to the student that underlines explicitly that the teacher sees the object as being lightly shaded. Wittgenstein remarks that this is a common and normal distinction of the language game of art expressing a recognisable quality of the art work, telling us what it is. By remarking that the student lightly shaded in the object there is the assumption that the student understands the concept (lightly shaded) connected to the sample (the perceiving quality of it) that as Wittgenstein remarks, the teacher has recognised correctly what it is and what is to be seen about the art with this particular quality attached to it. Wittgenstein further maintained that if the connection between the concept and the sample is recognisable then the comment by the teacher represents a *bona fide* aesthetic judgment with physiognomic meaning referencing the character of the student's object (Johannessen, 2004, p. 12). The illumination this gives being: 'the student lighted shaded in the object', is a meaningful expression of the student's art object's representation. When set in context, with or without further elaboration, it can turn out to be a valuable remark to make to a student that their object was 'lightly shaded'.

It is normal in the teaching of art to draw from, take note of and employ aesthetic and non-aesthetic qualities and phrases. Wittgenstein argues convincingly that we use non-aesthetic terms to express aesthetic reactions of the quality of an art: "you design a door and look at it and say: 'higher, higher, higher…oh, all right.' (Gesture) What is this? It is an expression of content?" (Wittgenstein, 1966, p. 13). But it is also, as Wittgenstein says, a move in the language game indicating that the door each time should be higher and higher, so that the higher and higher is expressing an action that it wants you to take. Therefore, there is something about the way we are using our language game in a situational task related manner that connects and explains our use of the word 'higher' about what should be done.

Lower it, higher it, move it to the right, stitch it here, feel this material, rearrange it like this, move your body this way rather than that way, play it like this, I prefer it when it was black rather than blue, the composition is just right, the dovetail joints on the chair are elegant are all instances of what makes the word or phrase in conjunction with the occasion-activity, an interjection of the kind of action, recognition and approval we are referring to (Wittgenstein, 1966, p. 2). Wittgenstein argues that we can verify things aesthetically by the language game we are using in many different ways. By pointing to what I see, making an interjection about what I see, explaining and seeing as, when I point to what I see, the pointing, the interjection, explaining and the seeing are verifying why it needs to be lowered, moved, bent, twisted, or seen as good, for example. "Red is something specific… but for that to be intelligible, one would have already to mean our concept 'red', to mean the use of that sample" (Wittgenstein, 1967, p. 60). We do not see the colour red (which is a gross colour like blue, green, yellow, black and white) by merely the concept of it becasue the the colour red when we see it is "tightly constrained by the physiology of the human visual system" (Hyman, 2006, p. 31).

Wittgenstein goes on to say in relation to art interjections and reactions that "it is the game in which these things appears in, not the forms of words" (Wittgenstein, 1966, p. 2) themselves that express the sense of things in particular ways. He is not implying that words do not matter, far from it, but rather that it is their use in a game-rule teaching situation (the game being an art production capable of expressing an understanding or a judgment that throws light on the perception-cognition of the use of the words and their intention in a universal, particular and singular way), of how to see it as, read it as, hear it as, and be able to carry it out. The particular language game used should be complete in itself to explain the associated aesthetic judgement and action that is being communicated. The language game when I write it down or express it gives reasons for supposing the correct way of how to 'read it like this' (Wittgenstein, 1966, p. 4) and 'what is wrong with this is that it is too long', for example.

The student knows what the teacher means by the words 'too long' in the teacher's conceptual use of it. While looking at the object themselves, they interject: 'I see this', upon which the teacher may go to explain further why it is 'too long'. To verify that the student sees that the object is 'too long' the teacher might ask the student to tell them why it is too long which would probably involve them expressing other concepts, or to draw, play and write what connects to the notion that the object is 'too long' in a contextually relevant, visual, written and performance manner. On their own, the words 'too long' may be too inexact. The language game of art is in proportion to the situations, processes, circumstances, culture and discipline-based art teaching occasions where it is appropriate to reveal why the art work is 'too long'. For example, this sentence is too long because the number of words you have used in it makes it difficult to connect the object with the subject; a music teacher remarks at the end of listening to a student playing their piece of piano music to them, that they should not hold down the F sharp and B flat notes for as long as they have done, but instead make the F sharp and B flat sound more snappy-short as the melodic pattern changes as the sheet music has indicated.

Students have to learn the rules of art because "if I hadn't learnt the rules, I wouldn't be able to make the aesthetic judgment. In learning the rules you get a more and more refined judgement" (Wittgenstein, 1966, p. 5). We can easily take for granted, as teachers, the difficultly that a particular language games poses for students, how difficult the 'particular' musical note, dramatic expression or dance movement, can be to imagine, carry out, be heard, be seen and be understood. For example, in order for students to understand the teacher's use of the word 'figure', it requires them to know, in general, that a human figure has two eyes, two legs and two arms. But we also know that in recognizing that this is a human figure drawn, other body parts and volumes are involved. What kind of view of the human figure might we want the students to draw (sitting down, a front view, a back view, a side view, laying down, in the distance and so on)? These are difficult tasks to express if one has not completed these kinds of exercises many times before. In recognising that the human figure has two eyes, two arms and two legs (with its other general body parts attached) is to recognise how such features will contribute to the image of the drawn human figure being seen as a human figure. The second part of the problem is how to express the eyes, arms and legs, for example, in a figuratively drawn, aesthetic, conceptual, posed way where such features come together so that our imagined minds, as Ernst Gombrich mentions, can picture the human figure as walking, gardening, sitting down, standing up, dancing and brushing their teeth. A lot of concepts, qualities and properties, building up an image that one wants to realise, where the surface and space understanding of the shapes, geometrical proportions, gestures and expressions are being altered each time before the final figure is reached, deploying different construction and modeling techniques and comparing what fits the image of the particular entertaining thought of the human figure that the student has in mind.

Drawing a human figure for the first time, as suggested, is a very difficult conceptual, perceptual, age-capability related and physically demanding task. There is a plethora of very complicated pedagogical teaching issues here. Yet, the difficulty is further compounded because the language games of art are flexibly applied to group situations and individual situations in creative ways, as Wittgenstein suggests, which can cause all manner of extra problems for the students of art. There are a myriad of incidents where, for example we might use the word 'lightly' without being precise about it, since on each occasion a scaffold of experiences relating to 'lightly' might be required to understand how on each occasion its validity presupposes what the quality is under each presentation. But prior action affects future action and understanding, as Wittgenstein (1969) remarks in his *Blue and Brown Book*. In art activity, experiences, pattern recognition, artistic developments, imagination and conceptual understanding with relevant samples shown, work together from simple to more subtle and complicated exercises of how to apply 'lightly' to many different art situational ways. Furthermore, Wittgenstein in *Zettel* remarks that 'lightly' is also characterized, as language games are, by what we do and what we cannot do with 'lightly' (Wittgenstein, 1967, p. 64). When a student learns to do something different with the word 'red' for instance, in an art class, they discover with the help of the teacher, that its matt effect is different from its gloss effect, opaque effect from transparent effect and that the saturation of a cadmium red will be become less intense or more intense by mixing it with a complementary colour or by adding, tones, tints and shades (black and white) to change the strength of the colour red that is being used.

Students learn in developmental ways to follow certain rules that begin at first in a language game with what they are commonly familiar with and then gradually, as Wittgenstein states, their intelligence and experience develops additional and extended uses of the associated language games of art. In an extraordinary number of different cases, the various judgments in the language games of art in education when we talk about correctness, knowledge, appreciation, conception and understanding in an art practice are founded on different premises of art. Wittgenstein suggests a teacher of art frequently wants the students "seeing this as that" (Wittgenstein, 1967, p. 37). This is to be noted because a teacher of art, for example, will explain what a metaphor is and show various examples of one. At some point they will follow this up by stating, 'now that you know what a metaphor is can you 'create' your own metaphor?' Wittgenstein refers to this process as verifying that the students know what a metaphor is. A music teacher says 'I want you to follow my clapping to this short melody as you are reading it in your music theory book…Do you think, having showed you the rhythm of this short melody, you can do the clapping on your own following the notes and pattern from the music theory book? Good, now let me hear you play it on the piano'. 'You have done a good job of drawing the object from a front view can you now draw the same object from the back view of it?'

"If a man goes through an endless number of patterns in a tailors and says: 'No. This is slightly too dark. This is slightly too loud', etc., he is what we call an appreciator of material. That he is an appreciator is not shown by the interjections he uses, but by the way he chooses, selects, etc. Similarly in music: 'Does this harmonize? No. The bass is not quite loud enough. Here I just want something different.' This is what we call an appreciator" (Wittgenstein, 1966, p. 7). The language games that a student or a teacher uses are an attempt to justify the seeing, hearing, conceptualizing, directing and feeling aspects as the student or the teacher plays this, does this, shows this, makes this, says this and explains this in order to state what is true about the art production, identifying aspects of the art that achieve its clarity.

Wittgenstein remarks: "supposing you meet someone in the street and he tells you he has lost his greatest friend in a voice extremely expressive of his emotion. You might say: 'It was extraordinary beautiful the way he expressed himself.' Supposing you then asked: 'what similarity has my admiring this person with my eating vanilla ice cream and liking it?' To compare them seems almost disgusting. (But you can connect them by intermediate cases.) Suppose someone said: 'but this is a quite different kind of delight.' But did you learn two meanings of 'delight'? You used the same word on both occasions. There is some connection between these delights. Although in the first case the emotion of delight would in our judgement hardly count" (Wittgenstein, 1966, p. 12). His criticism of the use of the words: 'expressive of his emotion' and I think the word 'beautiful' too as mentioned in the above quote relates to the previous paragraph's notion of 'seeing this as that', but in this case failing to do so. No particular identification is made that allows me to comprehend 'this' emotional delight and understand it.

Far too often, we over praise the geniuses of the art world over and above the simple but accumulative sophisticated productions of art that students produce and perform. The quality of art is in proportion to what a five year-old, an eleven year old, a sixteen year old and university graduate student of art can all achieve. Welfare maximisation overall is measured by what a five year old can achieve and by what older students can achieve through the different grade stages of art curriculum education.

Why are many of the basic things that are taught to students about art production so important to teach? There are many reasons why the basics aspects of art activity in any discipline ought to be taught but one of them I want to repeat is how Wittgenstein construes our use of how language games determine and recognise things. We take for granted, to repeat, more than we should sometimes, the aesthetically applied concepts of 'right', 'left', 'up' and 'down', 'the tempo needs speeding up', 'the spatial effects here' 'melody is part of our harmonic vocabulary in music', 'would lazy be a better word to use here instead of sleepy'. 'Seeing this as that', 'that is nice and soft', 'red and green are complementary' and 'the movement you see makes the gesture appear more loving', for example. How many times in an aesthetic way are such judgements made in and out of school? A fashion designer, product, automotive, graphic and furniture designer, a film maker, dancer, actor, jeweller, ceramist, architect, sculptor, photographer, musician and painter, for example, have serious recourse to such decision making language games in a variety of diverse, intricate and particular uses.

With background conceptual information supplied, we can know the reasons why the 'right' or 'left' and the 'up' or 'down' can make sense to us in an aesthetic thinking activity of art. In this direction-plane the object looks elongated but in this direct-plane the object looks elliptical. Accordingly, one of the concerns of art teaching is the students' acquaintance with such notional qualities of what 'left' and right' can explain and mean in an enormous range of different situations. Simply knowing ordinarily what 'left' and 'right' means, for example, does not explain why I want this X feature there or this space more open, closed at an angle and enlarged. Once the student has learnt a few of the applications of how 'left' and 'right' in art situations are deployed, they gain the confidence, familiarity and reassurance to know perhaps that there are lots of other ways we recognise how 'left' and 'right' are being used but only when we know their intentions. With further teaching guidance, the students, in learner-like situations, can observe and apply how 'left' and 'right' used 'this' way and 'that' way involve certain ideas, feelings and concepts relating to lengths, intersections, thicknesses, colours, textures and line qualities in particular spaces, volumes, proportions and with fabrics, metals, wood, clay, light, shadow, with movement, drama, music and in theories of art like De Stijl or in Paul Klee's writings on art.

Wittgenstein asserted that it was not the words we use *per se*, as the use we are making of them in language games. When the students are creating, for example, a visual intense pattern design around a theme, they might use the words 'right', 'left', 'up' and 'down' to expresses a difference, a reason and an identification that can give their arrangement meaning. It is also self-evident that we use such terms widely outside of artistic aesthetic considerations: 'take the next left to the airport', 'you were right about that', 'there is a lot of dumbing down going on here', and 'if it was up to me.'

"An object that has aesthetic qualities is an aesthetic object. They can be thought of as objects that have been made deliberately to have such qualities, qualities that we will find particularly interesting or meaningful. But other kinds of things can have aesthetic qualities and therefore can be aesthetic objects. For example, we often look at trees, mountains, pebbles, for their aesthetic qualities, that is, for how they look. Not only natural things but artifacts as well: city streets, automobiles, buildings" (Parsons & Blocker, 1993, p. 25–26).

Marion Richardson remarked that "in the happiest of the children's work I had learned to recognise a vital something" (Richardson, 1948, p. 14) and the evidence of the children's happiness as 'a vital something' is often the expression of their feelings, imagination, thoughts and ideas recognising, explaining and familiarising themselves with living representations of character, their secrets, their love of life and the strangeness of things they do not understand. Their lives, we know, are full of habitual association and the categorisation of events, objects and incidents corresponding to shared meanings as they see the world and experience it. They look about and ponder about their lives, they look about and worry about things, they look about and speak their minds, they look about and flutter their wings, they look about and are dazzled by sights and sounds and characters and scenery and they look about and wonder. The harmony of their lives relate to their poetic, imaginative experiences preserving a thought about a rainbow in the sky, of building sand castles on the beach, of what they know about people, the heaviness of their existence that might overshadow how they respond and engage, of the dances, melodies and rhythmic experiences that open them up and bind their humanity, bringing home to them their coherent safe or unsafe existence.

In connection to their immediate perceptions and contemplative estimates, the students are able to discern what will enable them to complete the art task through successive development that involves critical teacher dialogue. Involving incidents of 'this as that', explanations, intentions, observations, impressions, picturing, showing the action, justifications of why you did this, and gestures, for example, further the students' understanding and exhortation of their being in the world. This is not fluffy art activity thinking but what affects our making sense of the world in a general and in a social communicative way. What contains the student's overflowing experiences from the school playground, as it is displayed at home, as it is displayed by the five year old who at the end of a school day tells their mum and dad that their 'teacher was not nice to them today', as it is displayed when a new teacher enters the classroom and some of the students in the class will want to touch their hand and hold it, as it is displayed by one of the students asking the teacher 'what do you think of my drawing of this pig and do you think I have made the pig too fat', and when one of the other students asks the teacher, 'what did Tom Thumb mean in the Brother Grimm story that 'there is no place like home?' These are the impulses of social life and moral feelings, of higher culture evoking the students' imaginative aesthetic comprehensions, their pleasures and displeasures entertaining thoughts, ideas, feelings, perceptions and explanations that enable and furnish impressions of the student's life and their evidence of sense and understanding in their art that claims to see that, question that and justify that. A lot of learner-like activity is active.

To get the students further interested in art, a teacher may read an extract of Shakespeare's *Romeo and Juliet* followed by some of the students being assigned different character reading roles of the play where each takes it in turn in the class to read their lines up to scene two of the play (in one lesson). This teacher may ask the students to discuss amongst themselves in groups, the role the two houses (Montague and Capulet) play in the affairs of this story. The students may be taken to a musical concert of Beethoven's *Pastoral Symphony* and then later in the week have to discuss in class William Wordsworth's poem *The Daffodils*. This might be followed by a school visit to an art exhibition of John James Audubon's nature drawings and painting and then visit the school's nature garden to do some planting, raking and pH tests. In these four interconnected lesson plans, a fifth lesson plan is created leading to the students having to do a painting assignment, an essay, taking responsibility for the school's nature garden or producing a fashion garment around the familiar idea to the students of nature in winter, autumn, spring or summer but in ways they have not previously considered, engaging new activities, experiences, reflections, knowledge and creative thoughts.

"To pose aesthetic questions is to make the aesthetic experience itself more reflective, more critical, more resonant. Art education is deepened and expanded by what occurs in answering such questions" (Greene, 1995, p. 138). Indeed it is, but often to pose an aesthetic question involves imagining in an art-like learner way the visible, the reasoning, the performing, the conceptual and the readable. A student may be good at posing aesthetic questions but poor at aesthetic, media based, art construction activity. They may be able to ask the right questions but still not be able to take those steps to aesthetically create the evidence of achievement in performance and production. There is a correspondence between what the media-appearance of the art contains in it and the activity creation of it that connects to ideas exploiting different distinctions and theories about art. As Arthur Danto remarks when mentioning Bishop Berkeley's theory of mind: "what the mind contains are ideas, and ideas are just their contents, so the difference between a cow and the idea of a cow is not there to be drawn by Berkeley, who is after all eager to identify cows with the idea of cows" (Danto, 1981, p. 151).

Parsons and Blocker consider the qualities of an art production, like many of us do at times, in relation to the art's appearance in respect of features and thoughts dealing with the art's meaning and insight. The art's appearance and its meaning and insight overlap and supervene. Furthermore, if an art activity involves intellectual, practical, social and moral feelings, then naturally these will be determining causes of art. Similarly when the art is rhythmical, musical and decorative, the art's meaning and insight in an expressive-symbolic way could be interpreted as, loving, happy, melancholic and other sympathetic human feelings of life that we imagine to be peaceful, for example, Parsons and Blocker surmise that while we do enjoy the qualities of an art piece of work in a disinterested Kantian manner, we also "enjoy artworks as significant objects and part of their significance has to do with their complex relations with real life" (Parsons & Blocker, 1993, p. 30).

To say that 'a painting is beautiful' or to say 'wasn't that music performance very emotional', are, according to Wittgenstein, interjections of approval. But neither case explains what makes the painting beautiful or the musical performance emotional. So we don't know the quality of the art that induces the state of affairs and why it was beautiful or emotional. We have no way of understanding why the painting is beautiful and the musical performance is emotional. What we are going to need to do is to see the painting and listen to the musical performance in order to begin to understand why possibly the painting was beautiful and the musical performance was an emotional experience. "If I say of a piece of Schubert's that it is melancholy, that is like giving it a face (I don't express approval or disapproval). I could instead use gestures or dancing. In fact, if we want to be exact, we do use a gesture or a facial expression" (Wittgenstein, 1966, p. 4).

In the right situation the gestures, injections, expressions and actions we might use reflect what our aesthetic judgements might be: "If I like a suit I may buy it, or wear it often—without interjections or making faces. I may never smile at it" (Wittgenstein, 1966, p. 12). A smile, melancholy remarks, gestures, concepts and a dance are in the language games Wittgenstein uses and can be the correct aesthetic reactions that are part of the normal way we teach art. These reactions are serving situations within teaching that involve the art teacher's responses to an art teaching activity where the art teacher can point to the art work and have conversations about the art aesthetic habit forming connections that associate this musical, literay, painterly and design concept idea with its object.

We have seen what non-aesthetic features can express in language game aesthetic judgements. To rerun the issue, for example, "you could regard the rules laid down for the measurement of a coat as an expression of what certain people want" (Wittgenstein, 1966, p. 5). To support this position, Wittgenstein further mentions that the dress maker is able to make the precise cut to the precise length that is required. Hence, the dress maker determines the measurements that produces the narrow fit or the broad fit with its turned-up features on the cuffs and with the colour that the client asked for as signs of an aesthetic judgement. If we say that the arm length of a coat is impractical or the garment is too tight under the arms, then, maybe the language game we are using is non-aesthetic. However, it can also be seen that in this particular language game it could just as well be about aesthetic considerations. I am not going to want to wear something that is ridiculously too long for me or if I feel that the coat is uncomfortable to wear because it is too tight. In either case, I am not going to get much aesthetic satisfaction from wearing such clothing. The problem with assuming that the coat's measurements determine how pleasurable the coat is to wear, is to ignore the student fashion designers' concept design for the coat. Therefore, the pleasing aspect of the coat is not the measurements themselves but the coat itself, as it is the coat we are judging, not the measurements. The measurements reflect the coat design decisions that the student has produced. They would have had to take the client personal size measurements into consideration when designing the coat. But these are not aesthetic considerations but merely practical considerations which in due course will influence design aesthetic decisions. While the measurements may be tightened here and loosened there, for example, the design idea remains largely the same. The designer can tailor his or her design to the body measurements of their client. Something similar occurs in transport, product, furniture, architectural and interior design concept ideas.

It is the object we are judging that pleased us and that means first of all that it is definitely a coat we are seeing and not a pair of shoes. Saying it is a coat does not get anyone very far at all until aesthetically the student is able to particularise their concept design for a coat that the student envisages with the client in mind, since presumably the coat that the client wants is not like any other coat. Mentioning that the garment is a coat is not very illuminating about our taste judgments as it expresses nothing about the quality of any particular coat. A coat, the garment certainly is, but to the student designer it is an aesthetic object, a poetic expression of their talent, their creativity and their understanding of fashion and fashion trends. Wittgenstein is less than aware at times that the student designing the coat or any other fashion item we care to mention, what in Kantian terms can seldom be reached by the proposition: it is a coat. The love we have for this object does not come from the remark 'this is a coat' or 'cut the seam here on this dress'. I can admire the cutting expertise but not the dress design.

When Wittgenstein says the measurements by association express the aesthetic quality since the measurements are the rules for the coat designer, he has put to one side that the coat is the coat only because the student designer had an idea about the coat. The coat's idea is conceptually very important. What will the coat look like and upon wearing the garment what will it feel like? Isn't the owner of the coat expected to find delight in the coat's softness, lightness, warmth, toughness? This is a coat which might express an aspiration, a fantasy and a secret of ours. It may be that the coat we wear each morning to go work has no meaning for us; we take no delight from it other than a practical one. Yet, Wittgenstein has ignored that the fabric nature of the coat needs careful selection. He has not thought to mention that the thinness, heaviness, transparency, opaque and shiny surface of the coat with its turtle shape design pattern might matter to us. He has forgotten about buttons or other fastening systems that the coat has, he has forgotten the unusual but sensual features that the coat specifically might have, he has forgotten that the coat is a three-dimensional object, he has forgotten its colour or colours, he has forgotten its associations with nature, industry, liberty and how cozy it might feel, he has forgotten how dainty it is, and he has forgotten any practical features that the coat might have, for example. Now the measurement rules for the coat cannot provide for all of this. The measurements do not produce the design. We do not normally think from the measurements that it is going to be a wonderful coat rather, what we are aware of all the time would be the design of the coat. We are carrying around an image of the coat. Does it makes us feel part of a social group so that we blend in anonymously, or does it single us out while still feeling part of a social group? Certainly we know what the measurements and cutting patterns are doing, we known their intentions and the craftsmanship involved in it, what the different tools are used for that correspond to the cutting, shaping, sewing and pinning but let none of this obscure the fact that the design concept is responsible for all subsequent decisions and intentions and how everything ought to be made and look.

The measurements can, as Wittgenstein remarks, be an expression of the coat's aesthetic sense that relate to features of the coat. However this aspect alone, which can give pleasure both visually and in terms of comfort, is also a fashion object where the measurement not only feel right but they have been designed to exploit my shape, my height and my neck, for example. Any coat measurements have to be considered with more anatomical creative design decisions but still the measurements are not a complete account of the coat's sensuousness gnomic appearance and moreover the conceptual creative thinking that deliberately stimulated the design of the coat. In order to create the kind of art garment the student designer has envisaged for this coat, the sensuous, the conceptual and the practicalities of the coat design overlap to assert that the coat needs 'lengthening here' or 'shortening here', the merit or demerit of an aesthetically appraised adjustment that is in proportion to the student's concept design. The flaw in Wittgenstein's argument is not that non-aesthetic rules of a coat's measurements are important in creating the coat's shape and length and width and certain features, for example. It is more that the measurements only make sense when we know already what the coat in this instance is going to look like, when we can envisage it.

When the coat has the poetic quality in which we are able to take it in such a way that it lifts being in the world in an imaginative fashion, the place of our thought is within this experience. The fashion designer does not think in terms of the coats particular measurements until they can visualize their design, created an idea for it that will contain the measurements they want or the client wants. When we say it is too long we have to know that although the 'too long' is referring to an aesthetic judgement we do not know what that judgement is. For a fashion designer it was 'too long' because it reminded them of a trench coat that was just too much of a masculine throw back to the past, for example. Contained even in this remark is an aesthetic cognition, Wittgenstein would recognise, convictions about the kind of aesthetic quality the coat must not have. The student designer as much as the professional fashion designer has to be able to know what feeds his or her imagination, in order to produce a conceptually aesthetically designed coat that evokes, for the client, the full force of their fashion ideas.

Our students have to be able to imagine the coat in ways that they know what it will look like when finished because otherwise there are not any measurements. And yet there is nothing wrong in saying, as Wittgenstein does, that I give the client a picture of the coat to point out the highlights of it, the shape and its ambiance. The student designer is not selling measurements to the client or the person who is buying the coat. What they are selling instead is an aesthetic object. What the student designer is selling is an experience, an escape, an affinity with life and a feeling of coziness. The coat says, 'notice me' or 'don't notice me' and for the person who wears this coat, the art of the coat is saying something about them. The student designer is selling excitement, conformity, and anonymity. That this fashion garment is fun to wear: it is elegant, child-like, pretty, colourful, festive, dignified, sharp, fuzzy, glittering, and full of panache and delicacy, it's racy, youthful, and flashy. It is wild, extravagant, rugged, relaxing, nimble, mysterious, distinguished, seductive, bookish, rebellious, powerful, zestful, and unpretentious. There is no mention of the beautiful coloured pearl flowers and the plumages of the birds on the coat design with its hip belt. The garment is French, Italian, African, Aboriginal, Egyptian, Victorian, Jacobean, Art Deco, Punk, Futuristic, Surreal, De Stijl, Baroque, Faustian, Neo-classical, a battle of colour or a jazzy garment. It is curvaceous, airy, sweet, bashful, lilac, purple, decorative, professional looking, a style for a specific occasion, for work, office, sport, formal dining, clubbing, young and old and either a winter or a summer coat. These are the habits and the experiences that an art teacher teaches their students from an early age beginning with 'left' and 'right', 'red', 'lightly' and draw me a figure, for example.

If an art teacher declares, they can see how: 'delicately and lightly the student lightly shaded in their subject', an aesthetic quality judgment has been expressed by the use of the attributed adjective judgement that the object was delicately and lightly realised. Frank Sibley states that common aesthetic words (and we have seen quite a few of them previously expressed) are, for example: joyous, fiery, robust, dynamic, garish, stringent, tragic, sorrowful, powerful, brutal, serene, turbulent, gaudy, dramatic, chaotic, dainty, graceful, sensuous, peaceful, soothing, charming, sad, gay, taut, ugly, piquant, grand, felicitous, steamy, melodic, statuesque, rambunctious, disturbing, wonderful, intense, balanced, bold and handsome.

"On the one hand we say that a poem is tightly-knit or deeply moving; that a picture lacks balance, or has a certain serenity and repose, or that the grouping of the figures sets up an exciting tension; that the characters of a novel never really come to life" (Sibley, 2004, p. 127). Sibley argues that aesthetic concepts are not conditioned governed in the way that non-aesthetic features are (Sibley, 2004, p. 128) like square, pale blue, right and left, a light touch, and the speed of movement. We might agree with Sibley that "it is always possible for me to wonder whether, in spite of these features, it really is graceful, balanced, and so on. No such features logically clinch the matter" (Sibley, 2004, p. 132). Wittgenstein's reply might be that we use language games and that in these language games all sorts of combinations, permutations and creativity, in rule governed particular situational ways, determine my aesthetic thoughts, conceptual understanding, perceptions, delight or my aesthetic frustration with 'this as that'.

Clearly I have been explaining the variety of ways teachers of art can use aesthetic qualities in art educational situations. When judging students' productions of art, the teacher of art uses aesthetic qualities and propositions to define, explain, examine and conceptualise their ideas, concepts, feelings and thoughts. They will introduce their pedagogical artistic thinking that will include grammatical distinctions, art history, what the student has to consider, 'seeing as' and 'this as that' in relation to features, ideas, methods and actions, aesthetic concepts and their acts of estimation that will pin-point for the student how to move their work on. But I have been arguing that the activity of art in education engages the feelings of life connected to the elevated qualities of an intellectual, moral, aesthetic and socially expressed object or performance judiciouly instructive of impressions relating to common good in the world. Why aesthetic qualities are important are because they pronounce discriminatory, insightful and sensitive concepts and perceptual properties that relate to the students' art production for learning purposes. They are germane because the aesthetic quality of a drawing is characteristic of an art and the associations of the object's sensible relations under the students' imagination and conceptual analysis. The art's aesthetic qualities renders what is relevant and meaningful from what the student is drawing, playing, making, writing or acting in a class situation. Students discover what is worthwhile to express as an effort of their own minds, their imagination, physical actions and cognition that coextensively is creating the art's formal appearance in a music performance, drama or poem for example, in language games teaching ways. The students' powers of representation, conception or abstraction outwardly formed in the art production are also imaginatively construed expressions pleasing the judgement that the teacher of art makes in regard to the students production of their art.

Aesthetic language games relate to what is perceivable, what can be imagined and what can be carried out on the grounds that the art has 'this' aesthetic quality involving this idea, this thought, this admitting new movement. An aesthetic object having an aesthetic quality is explained by the features we perceive and the conceptual idea of the art work. The art works aesthetic quality corresponds to the way we experience 'this' quality, how it consists of 'this' quality possessing the cognitive and perceptual ways we can account for it. The art teacher discusses with the student their art characteristics and their feelings of life as judgements, impressions and ideas of their aesthetic understanding, appreciation, construction and expressive concerns.

In their discussions with art teachers, students in a class learn to appreciate that art production has aesthetic qualities and that they have to be able grasp how art production has aesthetic qualities; deducing, contemplating, realising, experiencing and deploying aesthetic qualities in a variety of ways as particular to their art activities and that of other artists in applicable situations. Aesthetic comment has to relate to the nature of the art activity. Affection for art involves our aesthetic experiences of an art and our ability to render the demands of an art in a communicative conceivable manner that is shareable.

In the art class as the teacher goes from desk to desk, stage to dance floor or from easel to easel, they show the students how the results of their constructions-actions generate aesthetic and non-aesthetic teaching comments that relate to each individual art student production, concept, idea, their looseness, their painterliness and their movement of the wrist that is always looking at their watch in a stage performance, making it possible that something is expected. An aesthetic public sense of the student art work is given that has attended to the individual, singular and particular object nature of the art enabling the student to derive, then and there, and on reflection, the efficacy of the teacher's remarks about their art.

With technology gaining so much ground in education generally, it still remains as true now as it ever was, that the teacher of art is an irreplaceable sophisticated figure of necessity in art education. Technology is no substitute for the human eye and ear and moreover, what teaching experience offers. In a classroom full of students, who has that suitable presence of mind to know how to motivate these students and get the best out of them? Who understands the classroom feelings that day, that hour, that moment? Who promotes the natural inclination of everyone in the class? Who is the most effectual person capable of consistently maintaining wellbeing in the class? Who understands, devotes and can provide those important learner-like situations where the feelings, thoughts and delights of the class are rewardingly and regularly being shared? Who reveals, and take part in the enjoyable moral sense feelings and transitions that occur in a classroom-studio-workshop environment? That the classroom is a moral good comes from the teacher of art maintaining teaching and learning standards and from the moral good that is indicative of the students in the class who take enjoyment from their class companionships, from the teacher who can ignite their understanding, is sympathetic and enables the students to realise the joys of learning.

I will further show in teaching ways how it is normal to refer to art education qualities that involve the learner-like language games of art that readily pay attention to aesthetic concepts of art and actions. What I want to portray now in a more situational, teaching manner, representing a realistic display over time, is the kind of concrete and regular student learner-like language games that do spontaneously occur in an art class that correspond to welfare maximization overall.

Let us imagine that the art teacher borrows from their grandad, who was an ornithologist, a large stuffed albatross. The art teacher has decided they are going to use this stuffed animal for a drawing-painting art class exercise over a three week period to a group of fourteen-to-sixteen year old students with considerable prior art experience. I have assumed that the art teacher has done their due diligence and done a lesson plan, consulted the art curriculum and that the art class is already fully underway and into the final week of drawing-painting this albatross. I have also assumed that the art teacher has discussed perhaps a little of the bird's habitat, geographical range, migration patterns, diet, aerodynamics and the dangers it faces.

Before I get to the actual, regular and normal comments we can expect an art teacher to make, that in learner-like ways are important in the teaching of art in ways that I have previously discussed, we have to bear in mind what the point of such an exercise is attempting to achieve. What might that be? Let us look at this issue first.

In no particular order: (1) we are going to want to be able to realise in student productions the aesthetic qualities of the students' drawings-painting of this bird that in learner-like ways correspond to what we ought to expect as a standard-benchmark quality of art from this age group. Therefore what are the heights of this art's understanding relating to this art activity and its outcomes that we can normally expect in a teaching way the students are reasonably able to grasp reflected in their production? What is the kind of evidence we would look for in their display that would correspond to this drawing and painting exercise revealing that the students had successfully produced what was required of them. I will discuss more about this a moment.

(2) How is this exercise contributing to a better understanding of life's social existence? This would relate to the forms of expression on display in the students' art productions. But what exactly are we looking to see that corresponds to showing signs of life in the art conjoined to knowing the sources of the attraction of the art, inducing social feelings for the art that the students have produced? The students' youthfulness exerting of themselves the character of the bird as we ordinarily can experience it and imagine it, of the deserved common empathy and feelings we have for the bird, of how there is vigor, excitement, pleasure, dignity, exuberance and understanding that has been portrayed. A good account poetically, that in socially shared imaginative ways so exhibited by the students is touching in its majesty in proportion to the students' capabilities. Not so differently, is it not also true to say that this teaching situation denoting students' observations, sensitivities, conceptions, experiences and imaginations of the associated expressed character of this art exercise is part of a developing process that is helping the student integrate into our world? For all of the above reasons, this art exercise represents what a lucid, artful and conceptual understanding of a bird through teaching instruction can achieve.

Isn't this also an exercise in a social way continuous with experience in art and life, expanding and advancing conditions that enable the realisation of the world around us of a wealth of thought, feeling and imagination that evokes part of our union with the world? Surely this is an art activity-experience capable of elevating one's cognition and feelings, our commonality of being in the world, with details and sentiments distinguishing our enjoyments and those sensitive currents that cultivate our sensibilities knowingly that are admiringly relevant and meaningful to express? This exercise surely has educational gravitas.

Our stuffed albatross is on a platform that stands in the middle of the class room with an array of suitable props around it. The art lesson, as suggested, is close to its completion. Thus what are the teaching comments that in learner-like ways would be construed as informative? 'You have caught the bird's pose in a very literary-naturalist manner. Do take a closer viewing of a few of Audubon's drawings, Albrecht Dürer's 1505 *Stag Beetle* drawing, The Lars Jonsson bird drawings (1990–2000s), Chen Zhifo (1862–1962) and Wu Zuoren's (1908) bird drawings, and Jack Shadbolt's several bird drawings (1960–1970s) that are all on the wall to your left, during your break time. Please do read on the same wall Samuel Taylor Coleridge's poem *The Rime of the Ancient Mariner* (1797–8). You might want to go the school library and take a look at Jim Dine's drawings or perhaps consider reading William Wordsworth's poem, *To the Cuckoo* as ways that can help you express more of the detail that you have already caught in this image'. 'You have incorporated in these overlapping drawings the bird's movement very convincingly, that I feel the bird is about to fly off triumphantly from the drawing page. Do however take a closer look at Yang Zhengxin's (1942) drawings on the wall opposite you during your break time who clearly experiments with new structures and in semi-abstract ways various relations you might consider exploiting for yourself'.

"You have spotted things well in this drawing, carry on with the gestural structural way you are drawing the albatross'. 'The frantic way you have drawn the bird in an agitated, aggressive manner is a perceivable quality of this bird that I can imagine'. 'The large, silhouette shape of the bird you have painted is very carefully constructed and has an elegance of controlled, emotional, image clarity we associate with the bird'. 'This is a lovely, formed image of the bird you have captured with a rich tapestry of personal colour choices in it'. 'You have produced a drawing that shows the bird unfazed by life which appears to represent your deep respect for the bird'. 'I liked the way you have imagined this bird to be perched on a branch of a leafless tree high-up on a rock face over a cliff's edge'. 'It is a dangerous looking wild image of a bird you have drawn'. 'This is a solid drawing that I have seen you do before in other art works, that desire to get the depiction looking just as it is'. 'A rare, detailed set of drawings of the bird's legs, feathers and feet showing some fine observations of its strength and fragility using a good range of tones and background highlights that help your composition show how you have used your observations as a scheme for your ideas'. 'In a imaginative manner you have captured the physical energy of the bird; was this inspired from some of the Haida art drawings from the wall opposite you?'. 'You have taken a gigantic step in pushing forward your colouring technique and with the washes and opaque paint areas bound up trying to catch the bird spirit past and present, there is a dream like quality to this work'. 'You show good measuring skills in this drawing that has enhanced the drawing quality, the accuracy and intensity of it'. The chiseling, sculptured feel of your mark-making corresponds well to the texture of the bird's feathers'. 'A romantic bird you have drawn, that has a kind of fragile quality to it'. 'A funny looking drawing of a funny looking bird produced in a compelling drawn fashion'. 'I like the decorative and symbolic manner you have interpreted this bird in a two-dimensional textile-pattern manner'. 'There is a lyrical, musical expression in the way you have drawn this bird that seems to be expressing what you feel about this bird'. 'A good use of thick and thin lines and shadows that are emphasising different features of the bird's body bringing out its majestic stance with moral feeling'. 'There is good action in the drawing conveying the bird's intricate movements'. 'The warm colours you have used with the sunset in the background of the bird are very relaxing on the eye'. 'This is a very muscular and powerful drawing'. 'The creature looks deliberately impish, feathery and frightened, was this deliberate?' 'What a sombre image you have drawn here'. 'A well balanced drawing with picture space, perspective and good layout and lots of volume that add an airy feel to the drawing'. 'It is fabulous'. 'I like the dark thunderstorm background and foreboding image you have drawn of the bird who seems to know what is coming'. 'What a very colourful and happy contented bird you have drawn'. 'Your use of thick black lines, a spot of paint here and there and all of it applied spontaneously with a distinguished beak for the bird that is particularly treated differently from other aspects of the drawing makes it a surprising, superior drawing from you'.

Not enough credit in education is given to recognising what an art teacher can achieve. The language game communicated in the above paragraph from this teacher of art is purposeful, rich, instructive, conceptual and meaningful. The teacher's comments are socially relevant because they can be seen as part of a developing cognition, perception, imagination and an idyll of ordinary, connected life, which as Iris Murdoch mentions, reveals how art pierces the veil of appearance to further give sense to a greater notion of reality, a source of good energy, she says, that when so armed as I describe above: "suddenly I observe a hovering kestrel. In a moment everything is altered. The brooding self with its hurt vanity has disappeared. There is nothing now but kestrel. And when I return to thinking of the other matter it seems less important" (Murdoch, 1997, p. 104). What has been effective in this series of art lessons, in a publicly spirited, pedagogical manner, amidst the rigors of art teaching, is a superior good, representing the coming together of different ways to conceive of the bold, delicate, moderate, eye-catching and imaginative work that is of a general benefit to society.

There is an enormous amount of required attention, intellectual and perceptual involvement and reflection as dialectic in the aesthetic qualities of an art that a student expresses in their art productions. Viktor Lowenfeld and W. Lambert Brittain state, "each drawing reflects the feeling, the intellectual capacity, the physical development, the perceptual awareness, the creative involvement, the aesthetic consciousness, and even the social development of the individual student" (Lowenfeld & Brittain, 1987, p. 59). For a younger age group, the aesthetic qualities of an art begins to be learnt the moment one gives the student a brush in their hands, a musical instrument to play, a piece of music to listen to, a range of fabric or timber to cut, join, bend and glue or an instruction to 'dance like a seagull', for example. Getting used to and understanding progressively aesthetic qualities in learner-like ways involves those further moments when the art teacher comments: 'to give the drawing more balance you need to.', 'this needs more colour intensity to brighten it up' 'this drawing needs less vibrant colour and vivid mark-making in the background so that we can see better the figures you have drawn' 'the figure drawing is too small in comparison to the house behind the figure' 'the blue colour area in your painting needs to be darker because.', 'can you tell me about your composition'?, 'if you put a square shape here to replace the existing round shape here, do you think that it might create a better stronger pattern to your design?'

Inventive and stereotypical drawing and painting exercises are two common ways students learn to express aesthetic qualities whether they be stick-like exaggeration figure proportions, or with the use of plenty of symbols representing all manner of things that we have to think about as teachers with a young five year old child's square making ability. The child's capabilities obviously underlie and consist of the conditions that enable art experience to flourish, making judgments that correspond to the formal conditions of an art activity, the lesson plan and what the student is capable of achieving. Knowing that a student between the ages of five and six can draw plenty of geometrical shapes calls for much lesson planning (Lowenfeld and Brittain, 1987, p. 47) that is clearly not comparable to the same kind of lesson planning at university level teaching of art, yet hardly different from it either.

A music teacher might say to their students when playing the piano: 'is this sound different from this sound and how is it different, can anyone tell me?', 'is this a high note or a low note', 'is this sharp or soft', and 'does this sound tinny to you?', 'am I walking or running as I play this tune', 'which is more melodic my playing this or you playing this?', 'does this sound scary to you' and 'does this sound like 'I am in love?', 'does this remind you of a train and if so why does it?', 'what gives it that register in the music?', 'is the harmonic tones that you hear, the rhythm or the cadence or is it all of these things together?' Aesthetic quality is further revealed in an art lesson, as Sibley mentions, when the teacher begins to introduce to the children: "that simple pieces of music are hurrying, or running or skipping or dawdling, from there we move to lively, gay, jolly, happy, smiling or sad, and as their experiences and vocabulary broaden, to solemn dynamics, or melancholy. But the child also discovers for themselves many of these parallels and takes interest or delight in them. They are likely on their own to skip, march, clap or laugh with the music, and without this natural tendency our training would get nowhere" (Sibley, 2004, p. 138).

Sibley further points out that the artistic language games that are used by "critics and commentators [and teachers of art] may range, in their methods, from one extreme to another, from painstaking concentration points of detail, line and colour, vowels and rhymes, to more or less flowery and luxuriant metaphor. Even the enthusiastic biological decorated with suitable epithet and metaphor may serve.

What is best depends on both the audience and the work under discussion" (Sibley, 2004, p. 137).

In a Wittgensteinian manner, "an appropriate gesture may make us see the violence in a painting or the character of a melodic line" (Sibley, 2004, p.137). Likewise, as Sibley mentions, it often helps in teaching "to talk around what we have said, to build up and supplement the art experience and concepts with more talk of the same kind. When someone misses a swirling quality, when one epithet or one metaphor does not work, we throw in related ones" (Sibley, 2004, p. 137). These teaching principles are well known and are adhered to.

A few more thoughts about social values expressed in art education teaching ways need, I feel, widening. To ensure that the aesthetic qualities of an art production represents, as Dewey certainly thought, the associations continuous with ordinary and common life in socially, evolving, creative ways involves, most definitely, our human sympathetic feelings, as Mill mentions thoughtfully, addressing our lives in the world, as manifestations of our emotions, tenderness, joy, business lives, frames of mind, conceiving the beauty of flowers, the meadow, music or persons, moral ideas and choices in life, for example. It is by way of acting, playing, making, writing, performing and in other associated forms along with the continuing process of common and ordinary life, of observations and experiences that can form the schema of ideas with intrinsic worth and amplitude, that the aesthetic qualities of an art concerned with human beings existence and adoptable to all kinds of ends in education, meets with our approval. As a result, art activity in education strikes a chord with the behaviour, articulation and interests of life or what Wittgenstein called, the living. For Sibley to be able to create art means further having to point to and additionally discussing the key features of the art qualities that have a bearing which assists the educational development of the student aesthetic understanding of art. In an educational manner, aesthetic understanding for Sibley involves: "(1) what natural potentialities and tendencies do students have (2), and how are they developed taking advantage of these capacities in training and teaching" (Sibley, 2004, p. 138).

Educationally, what are the natural-social tendencies, capacities and teaching aspects of an art that will bring us to see aesthetic qualities and make us feel invigorated by them, use them, apply them, appreciate their relevance and justify them in agreed ways? This must be part and parcel of what a student habitually thinks, what they can appreciate and what they are capable of achieving, where the growth of a young sudent's aesthetic understanding of art is on "an ever changing continuum" (Lowenfeld & Brittain, 1987, p. 102). A young student, Wittgenstein remarks, first learns to apply a word like 'good' to food, to a painting they have done of their parents or their goldfish and dog, their home and a holiday for example. "One thing that is immensely important in teaching is exaggerated gestures [characteristics, properties, movements and sounds] and facial expressions" (Wittgenstein, 1966, p. 2).

What child doesn't like in a social way, dressing-up to role play and act out an incident indicative of their environment around them; doesn't like visiting a museum;

doesn't like playground activites, house or garden games; doesn't like finger and hand painting, singing in tune with the piano in a class; doesn't like holding a spider in their hands, playing with toys and doll's houses and being read stories. These are amongst some of the most commonest and inspiring ways we combine and extend our literal and imaginative activities of social life, which we put to use in our stories.

We know that Charles Dickens, for example, regularly walked the streets of London in search of characters, accents, idioms, conversations and incidents. The streets of a city or a small town are full of human accounts, representing the picturesque and the fantastical that are the ripe pickings for fictional inspiration. What an art teacher is interested in is "how we shift from literal to aesthetic concept uses" (Sibley, 2004, p. 138)? Andrew Sanders mentions of Dickens how "his delight in words began early. He later recalled being fascinated as a boy in the blacking-factory by the effect of seeing the words "COFFEE ROOM' reflected backwards as 'MOOR EEFFOC' the shifting quality of words and meanings remained important from Bill Stumps's mark in Pickwick Papers to Durdles's epitaphs in Edwin Drood" (Sanders, 1986, p. 549).

The impulse to shift from the literal to the aesthetic (as Dickens shows us above) is a naturally occurring phenomenon when the snare drum beats a rhythm in an act of celebration, when we hear the whistle of a train, play the recorder in class, spontaneously wiggle and jump and play hop-scotch in the school's playground, feel the prick of a rose thorn on one's finger, hear the creaking of a door and see a humming bird feed. When we notice how water distorts objects in a glass, when we put a broom stick between our legs in order to gallop like a horse, when we see how a snake crawls and hear how it hisses, pulls out its tongue and lifts its head. The student watches a programme on television on space and decides instantly to build themselves a cardboard box spaceship so that they can sleep in it at night, feeling enriched by their imagination of space adventure. In the day time a class of young students on a field nature trip skip through the daffodils on the hill in order to study the frogs in a local pond. From Standhal's autobiography "in which the author evokes the first-insignificant-notices that marked him as a child: ringing church bells, a water pump, a neighbours flute."Stendhal testifies to an aesthetic regime in which the distinction between those things that belong to art and those that belong to ordinary life are blurred" (Rancière, 2009 p. 4–5). Shakespeare certainly knew how to blur life and art together; a trade mark of many an artist's work but more to the point, it is what ordinary people practise too in their lives.

It is in the familiar, ordinary and commonly shared experiences of life that the similarities, contrasts and opposites between things begin to be explored, developed and imagined in educational practices of art. A triangle and a circle, a high note and a low note, something warm and something cold, something fast like a cheetah and something slow as a sloth, what is opaque and what is translucent and from random marks to more organised marks and back again can be the stimulating, explorative exercises for students representing complete and significant answers about our world.

A PARADIGM CASE

Parsons and Blocker

The narrowly utilitarian character of most elementary education, and the narrowly disciplinary or cultural character of most higher education.

(John Dewey, 1944, p. 136)

What I am going to examine now is a paradigm art educational case study. The case study involves one particular thirteen year old student that Parsons and Blocker interview. At the heart of Parsons and Blocker's teaching approach is their remark that 'we understand people well only when we understand the assumptions they make'. Parsons and Blocker explore an art teaching incident based on some common student assumptions that crop up regularly in an art class teaching situation to reveal aspects of a student's understanding of art, that correspondingly becomes a substantive teaching issue to address.

It is not necessary for me to fully articulate all possible discussions we could have for further promoting a better understanding of art in education around the incident that Parsons and Blocker expand upon. I am going to present enough of the reasons why the Parsons and Blocker approach is representative of good teaching practice in art.

Just how sophisticated art teaching can be is spelt out to us in one way by these two educational writers. Their approach to teaching art under such given circumstances corresponds to their interviewed thirteen year old's particular assumptions. For Parsons and Blocker, this is a quality teaching issue in art education and drawing from it, they devise subsequent art class exercises arising out of it aiming to tackle further student assumptions conjoined to opening the way for a better understanding of art and life.

The point I am raising and why I have chosen this Parsons and Blocker example, has to do with how their thinking and resource based suitable materials-exercises concerns aspects of the quality of art and student thinking about art determining the attending teaching facilitation which, in all probability, produces the desired positive effect, because of the attention given to the issue, on the art class production and understanding of art. The approach they take would seem also to meet the challenge of welfare maximisation overall. It is exactly a situation like this, that suggests why teaching is fundamentally important when understanding students' outlooks and in response, promoting directly the higher qualities of an art in social, aesthetic, intellectual and moral thinking ways. Students' assumptions, for our two educational practitioners, represents students' consciousness of art that needs addressing in the teaching of art for reasons that relate to student progress in art production and understanding. The teaching resources and the way Parsons and Blocker discuss an art teaching concern, correlates with the kind of human proof required for acceptable welfare maximisation overall.

Parsons and Blocker interview a thirteen year old student called Debbie, who has been asked to discuss her thoughts about Ivan Albright's 1930 painting: *Into the World Came a Soul Called Ida.* Parsons (1987) previously discusses this painting briefly in his book *How We Understand Art,* with the same Debbie but expands upon it further in Parsons and Blocker's book *Aesthetics and Education* (1993). I am taking their example because I believe it is a common enough and a good enough example of a teaching and learning issue in art education that is still relevant today. The first thing I want to emphasize in my analysis of this case study is how Debbie's response exhumes quality itself for teaching purposes. Her perceptions represent why teaching is relevant, or to put it another way what would go amiss without it. Debbie's thoughts about this Albright painting are what arguably serve the providence that affects superior teaching in art. This case study incident involves on the one hand what the teacher is capable of learning from Debbie's assumptions and on the other hand what subsequently, in lieu of her assumptions, they should execute in respect of their thinking that is capable of improving students' understanding of art. At issue, fundamentally, is the teacher realising that there is a problem that needs attention in order for progress in art to be made.

The problem that Debbie has with the art work she has been asked to comment on, is eminently proper to the core values of teaching art. Debbie is very honest in giving her opinion and one of the commanding concerns for teaching art is that the teacher ought to be very interested in what Debbie has to say and appreciate it substantially because this is what affects teaching in art. In this instance of teaching art, Debbie's cognition matters because it enables the teacher of art to decide what to do next to advance her understanding of art. The teacher appreciates Debbie's comments because now they can see what the problem is. Therefore, Debbie has presented an art teaching quality issue that, having recognised it, influences a good teaching strategy in art education that can subsequently be devised for it. A teacher of art who is unable to recognise that Debbie has presented a quality teaching issue will have failed to see that Debbie's assumptions will not go away and sooner or later in a variety of different ways will resurface until educational attention is paid to this issue. The art teacher, of course, may recognise that this is something they should address but may judge quite properly that this is not the moment to do so. Even having recognised that there are learner-like concerns here, time constraints and a curriculum packed with lots of topics to cover before the year is out, may provide little space for the teacher of art to address Debbie's outlook, limiting what a teacher realistically can achieve.

Certainly we might think that in selecting this painting *Into the World Came a Soul Called Ida,* would raise a host of normal art, social, moral and intellectual issues about the painting. Debbie, who is only thirteen years of age, is just beginning to comprehend these issues more self-consciously. The fact that she is beginning to become more aware of these issues is also the time perhaps educationally through exercises to try to advance her own thoughts on these matters more reflectively and appreciatively. Debbie has presented the teaching profession with a quality reason why teaching is important in art and in connection how the teacher of art is going to teach art in a potentially beneficial manner.

Presenting classroom exercises relating to notions of beauty and ugliness in the world has to do with our continuing social fascination and modification of different construed ideas of what constitutes the image messages that these notions are capable at once of being comprehended in a community; noting what students think, feel and imagine for themselves, of how art can condition our thinking about beauty and ugliness. Parsons and Blocker devise tasks where the contentions of beauty and ugliness, from examples in the community from past and present art evidence, can be discussed in social, aesthetic, moral and intellectual ways in a class.

However, it also seems necessary that in these discussions one does not just widen student understanding of these important topics resting upon different commercial interests, equality issues and different artistic positions. But equally, I feel, in at least some of the art task activities and in some of the corresponding related discussions, there should be a concern in the art teaching capable of dealing with how the intellectual, social and the moral delight of an art's imagery-performance in the world can be compatible with normal higher expressions of delight and why these normal higher expressions of delight are good for us. Therefore, there should be a three pronged approach: to discuss the ordinary higher aesthetic experiences from an art that we feel deeply and communally indebted to because the art's insights are good for us; together with how an art aesthetic delight is the effectuation of the representation within the art's presentation as our estimate of the art; and thirdly that there are social, intellectual and moral issues related to notions of beauty and ugliness in the world that affect being in the world. In addition, we also strengthen and differentiate, in other ways through different projects, exercises and assignment work, how to reach an accord by means of sense of how we take refuge and pride from our social ties of life that are good for us. It is immensely valuable for art education to develop a strong interest in the delights of our artistic freedoms that unite and explore the depths of our common typical actions and conversations that make it known the perceivable, associated, ordinary acts of our existence we prize. Where the beauty of the art preserves in intellectual, moral and aesthetic alliances reaching the eye, the ear, the performance and the cognition solidly, and of how differently, ugliness disturbs and threatens moral, intellectual and aesthetic delight while still, of course retaining aesthetic delight in how art production portrays the ugly.

Parsons and Blocker ask three questions which Debbie responds to as follows:

1. *What do you see in this painting by Albright?*

There's a lady sitting in a chair with her legs exposed. They're bare and they're really ugly. They've got bumps all over them and she's sitting there with a powder-puff in one hand and a mirror in the other. She sort of looks like a witch.

2. *What's the feeling in the painting?*

I don't know. It's just that the legs are getting on my nerves.

3. *Why do you suppose the painter painted it?*

He was angry with his mother-in-law (laughs). I don't know. He just felt like it. He saw some lady going down the street and he said: 'That looks sickening,' and so he decided to paint her. He was angry at her for some reason. (Parsons & Blocker, 1993, p. 87)

Apart from the fact that questions 2 and 3 above appear a little ambiguous, students in an art class will likely have different opinions about this Albright painting and some students will make more insightful comments than others about this painting. Yet this is a pedagogical situation, so anything a student might remark upon can be, in learner-like ways, insightful and moreover aren't Debbie's comments somwhat typical of a thirteen year old? Parsons and Blocker surmised that Debbie's response to this painting reveals her assumptions about beauty and ugliness in the world. Although Parsons and Blocker do not discuss much of this painting itself, or the perceivable qualities of it as an aesthetic and painterly issue in itself, it is clear that primarily they are concerned with Debbie's cognitive reactions.

They see Debbie's response as a legitimate basis in which to explore, as a consequence, teaching and learning issues in a classroom manner with students, examining beauty and ugliness in artistic, social and moral thinking ways. Before we get to that, we know that we could draw up a range of alternative questions to do with this painting by Albright that could additionally extend what Parsons and Block have asked Debbie to respond to. The three questions that Parsons and Blocker have asked Debbie to consider are common, regular, quality questions of art in education. These questions have to do, of course, with getting to know what Debbie's response is: her attitudes, her interest, her perceptions and her beliefs. Needless to say, the extent of Debbie's artistic experience and insight is indicated by her assessment of this Albright painting.

Nevertheless, I feel we have to be a little cautious here about Debbie's response. Debbie's communicating thoughts about the Albright painting may not represent what she is more able to communicate in a painting or in a possible sketchbook she has produced. The motives of our mind, imagination, feelings and cognition can work in an entirely different way, to produce that which in an appearance we could value most dearly. Might Debbie feel she is more adventurous and insightful, more enlivened, penetrative and at peace with herself when expressing the depth of her sensibility and sensitivity through an art activity production of a visual kind than with rational, grammatical words and sentences alone? It could be that words and verbal reasons deprive her of representing her true self and her true talents, where in a Kantian manner, an object in art freed of "conformity in law in the empirical employment of judgement generally" (Kant, 1928, p. 31), can instead come from the student's spontaneous free play cognitive faculties that affect and transform the way the object is created, while at the same time being concerned about the physical properties of the object as it develops. Debbie's own peculiar and contingent imaginative and cognitive responses can express in the end production of her art, her own purpose that has the kind of quality that is her mode of representation, introducing into the figure of art as a consequence more of herself into the work rigorously exhibiting a sophisticated piece of art work. It is not always the case that those who can produce convincing arguments are those who can produce the best art and are those that know more about art and the world. The Lascaux Cave painters were illiterate but incredibly intelligent perceivers of life and of aesthetic understanding in the world.

Parsons and Blocker's interview questions concern the spectator's point of view but a danger with this view, which the authors do not fall into, is whether enough of a spectator's points of view have considered the aims and intentions of the artist. Furthermore, to repeat Danto, what affects reasons in art is how sometimes there ought to be a correspondence that we can recognise between what the media-appearance of the art contains in it, through which ideas are further given. That appearances matter is one way how we can understand things and Wittgenstein, for example, in *Zettel* (1967) and *Culture and Value* (1980) gives plenty of examples to this effect.

The exercises that Parsons and Blocker discuss are concomitantly designed to extend Debbie's and other students' understanding of the notions of beauty and ugliness in art and life. The effectiveness of these exercises can be assessed ordinarily by the teacher of art. To ask whether Parsons and Blocker's teaching methods are meaningful for an art class to tackle, depends on what we know about the students' capabilities, the suitability of the exercises, time constraints and the teacher's art educational experience. Since Parsons and Blocker already know what Debbie thinks of Albright's painting, it is further possible, given Parsons and Blocker's suggested teaching materials, to assess for change in cognizance coinciding with perceptions coupled to these exercises.

Parsons and Blocker deserve much credit as they suggest several reasonable ways of how "one might get students to collect and categorise images of people and things that they think are beautiful and ugly and that have been thought beautiful and ugly in the past" (Parsons & Blocker, 1993, p. 88). The point of this exercise is for the students in the class to collect and display a broad range of images consisting of cultural, feminist, gender, commercial, social, moral, historical, idealistic, ancient, traditional, contemporary and conventional standards of how beauty and ugliness has been disseminated, accepted, interpreted and have contributed perhaps to problems in our society. Furthermore, Parsons and Blocker suggest, "getting the students to see that Ida the painting is not an ugly work, though Ida the person may be. Students can be brought to read the painting as a sympathetic interpretation of Ida's state of mind. Ida's suffering is brought rather forcefully to our attention and is thereby made significant, and what the viewer should be preoccupied with is Ida's sense of loss of youth and attractiveness and hence dejection and hopelessness. This is a view of the work that will often strike students quite powerfully and will transform their response to it" (Parsons & Blocker, 1993, p. 89). Therefore, attitudes to the art work involve students' life experiences, perceptions and conceptions of art and their receptiveness to it.

It could equally be supposed, as I think the authors might accept, that Ida (the figure in the painting) is attractive. Would we accept that Ida, in an imaginative way, might see her inner beauty as transforming her external appearance? Are appearances deceptive? But if appearances are deceptive could Ida's view of herself also be deceptive? Isn't it also the case that an art work's external appearance can express something life giving about its own appearance that may also be deliberately about an internal associated consciousness of the human figure in art making full use of its external appearance to suggest this? In seeing herself as beautiful should society go along with this in a positive way? When Ida the figure in the painting looks into a mirror and reflects on what she sees of herself, might she be reassured about herself? That one can take delight in old age has a beauty in itself? Mimetically the cracks and lines in the face of Ida as portrayed in the painting, for example, are perhaps as they should be as one gets older and are what we might come to expect. If mimetically such features seen are common enough, they are there as a truth of life that can have its own poetry, its own sophisticated voice, its own argument of pleasure, its own rightfulness, reality, goodness and moral value. A painting that shows things as they are, even if the painting is troublesome, means the painting is not necessarily the problem, but society could be and vice versa the painting could be if it is deemed offensive. But if we believe that this Albright painting is offensive, who is it offending, was this the intention of the artist, and how is it offensive and in what way? Is it degrading, abhorrent, disgusting, dangerous and shameful, for example, to the nation, to Ida, to you, your parents and the class? Are our reactions to the painting befitting of the painting, that the painting has intrinsic worth because this is now things are in the world of interest to human health? Does the painting require a sense of free judgment perhaps, does it have good intentions, is it part of a liberal point of view, does it raise issues worth discussing without exerting undue influence, provocation and serious challenge? Should art be conservative and contrite? These are the sorts of questions that can further students' understanding of what art is.

That any human being at whatever age is a beautiful human being to behold is a moral, social, intellectual and aesthetic argument. The mimetic artistic argument might also maintain that if we cannot look and enjoy the possible sweetness that is there to behold, our aesthetic sensitivity is limited, if not contradictory, since age is not a factor when we admire at times, certain famous celebrities, politicians, novelists, scientists, sports men and women, adventures and mountains, old trees, old cars, old clothes and old plays. If we knew that Ida had done amazing things in her life, was an inventor, on Broadway, a famous film star, broke a dozen sports world records, and found a cure for a disease which she got a Nobel Prize for, would we look at her differently in the painting and would we want to meet her? If, on the other hand, we found out that she spent all her life working in a factory and that she left school at fourteen years of age because she had to support her family would this also change our view of her?

The fragility of life may be the idea that Albright, in this painting, wants us to notice. Is beauty skin deep and does it have a shelf life? Don't we need art, more to the point, to externalise who we are and to find in it, as André Comte-Sponville mentions, a reflection of ourselves (Comte-Sponville, 2005, p. 100)? The painting is a reflection of ourselves in the world, the human species, is perhaps one argument. And if we do not see a reflection of ourselves in such an image, become aware of ourselves when viewing such a painting or come to be unaware of ourselves as a consequence of the painting, something pleasing, thoughtful or stirring and of something missing perhaps, as Comte-Sponville goes on to say, are we then seeing something absent of man or woman? What humanity is there being expressed in this Albright painting? If physical beauty is easy to look at, it is cultural and social. Can an artist depict a man or woman who looks old as easy to look at too? Art, Comte-Sponville mentions, "helps us perceive and to inhabit the real life" (Comte-Sponville, 2005, p. 106).

We know that there are a lot of different ways to teach art and that different property, ideas, cultural identities, movements and techniques can be classified stressing the type of art it is. The quality of teaching and learning is a two way process: the teacher sees something or hears something and the student sees something or hears something too, but what the student sees or hears may be misinterpreted or not understood well by them. Teaching quality involves student learning problems and those accompanying regular teaching moments in a class that confirm that the students 'gets it'. 'Getting it' is a necessary teaching concern and not 'getting it' may call into question the teaching approach.

It is feasible that the person behind the painted image by Albright, as Parsons and Blocker indicate, might be a cynical manipulative human being but nothing in this painting indicates this. Perhaps in the painting we don't see Ida as suffering at all. Do we really need to judge her? In fact, how can we judge her when we do not know her? There is no way of knowing from the painting that the painting is making a character judgment about her. If we feel uncomfortable with the painting as Debbie seems to, then are there moral and social issues worth drawing out? Is this painting deliberately intrusive, unacceptably so, like some reality TV shows are? Is the painting sufficiently representative of whom Ida is in appearance in this cameo representative artistic manner? Certainly this might be Ida as she is in appearance in a representational artistic manner, but is this what Ida always looks like? Do we think Albright wanted to paint a flattering image of Ida? Could any painting ever be sufficiently representative of any person? Is our notion of human beauty related to our friendships in life, to the body, the culture and the face we are born into, to intellectual status or financial success or character and moral action in life? Is the way we see Ida representative of her community and her age group? What human sympathetic feelings of our moral spirit might we express here embracing Ida fictionally? Is Ida a human being in a world and is that what the painting is suggesting? If this is the case, would it change our view of the painting? Should we censure such paintings? Have the students in the class noticed how commonly "the idea of beauty is used in talking about people [landscapes, the built-environment, mathematics, philosophy, politics, friendships, deeds, actions, and objects] as much as in talking about art" (Parsons & Blocker, 1993, p. 90).

Another issue is the idea that "a painting could not be beautiful if it pictured my old and rusting automobile" (Parsons, 1987, p. 39). Many Romantic poets and painters took inspiration from ancient and monastic ruins, dilapidated buildings and from fog polluted cities. What is it about an image seen in the flesh if Ida the painting was printed on a large billboard in the centre of one's town, what might our reaction to it be? It would also be worthwhile to consider the similarities and the differences of how music, literature, a play and a building can make us also alive to the beautiful and the ugly.

Aristotle believed we take pleasure from a drama's tragedy because we can experience the positive quality of the drama's art production. Where the positive quality is apparent in the moral, aesthetic, social and intellectual shared imaginative experiences and feelings that are proper to the art's cause, the art brings forward what is relevant about the tragedy, in how it succeeds in its tension, familiarity, relaxation, darkness, mental ordeals and real grief, where appreciatively what takes place is interpreted to be the correct human response. The art renders what is realisable in experience, coming into an accord with our cognition and perceptions, the attraction of the art's incidents and scenes imaginatively perceived and drawing out its terror, danger, helplessness and despair as we can imagine life so construed in such circumstances and situations to be.

Plato stated that beauty could be a physical-bodily attraction while also remarking that beauty was in proportion to intellectual and moral truth and goodness. Is beauty one of love rather than in appearance, 'good looks' *per se*? Should we see our human beauty, the depth of it in connection to the world around us, in what, Haida culture, for example, would argue should be in harmony with the vegetation, forests, rivers, mountains, flowers, fish, birds and land animals? Is beauty, as Kant seems to have suggested, "a contemplation of nature or art that produces a 'satisfaction without any interest'. The pleasure ('satisfaction') we find in beautiful things is completely independent of their relations to the rest of the world—of their uses and effects"

(Nehamas, 2007, p. 3). How might a teacher of art show these differences to students in a class and discuss them?

While Debbie's thinking is not necessarily representative of all her classmates, it is representative of one normal view of a mixed ability class of students. How to overcome Debbie's perceptions and understanding about the Albright painting while catering to the needs of the whole class, involves the whole class being open to new conceptions, reasons, causes, realities, possibilities, intentions and relations on how the students see beauty and ugliness in the world, sharing their responses through the exercises and discussions which are designed to stimulate and develop in superior ways the students' artistic understanding in an art class commensurate with the class capabilities and their limits of cognition.

We could go back to Debbie and assess whether her views concerning the beautiful and the ugly have changed as a consequence of Parsons and Blocker's envisaged teaching exercises. But all devised teaching exercises stand lifeless and inert. Until there is considerable representation, interaction and engagement from the students, nothing can be accomplished. The dynamics of the class, the contingency that is emphatically caused by their spontaneity and all manner of their human responses in the class representing individually and collectively substantial different modes of reactions constitues the life perceiving, conceiving and realising that makes things achievable. This is the essential foundation of teaching. The intelligent actions of the art teacher begins by embracing these facts of life, not denying them, when organising, motivating, explaining, realising, reflecting, convening and discussing, leading to the adoption of the best teaching facilitation that advances students' understanding and capabilities. It is very likely that Debbie's understanding of art would have advanced as would reasonably be expected given Parsons and Blocker's comprehensive sense of the art teaching issues involved valid to the concerns that we know will make a difference. Effective teaching is what serves as a basis for leaner-like understanding, the apprehension of the things that are concurrent with teaching exposed to the student reading-performance of the different judgements the students make about an art and their art production. Discussing with the art class their own thoughts when undertaking these exercises will enable the students to recognise and appreciate the insights and actions that will fruitfully move students' art work forward in the direction that will show development in the art task. There is an ethic of care in Parsons and Blocker's approach that speaks volumes about the quality of art and the quality of teaching and learning in art.

ARE ALL AESTHETIC PLEASURES EQUAL?

Never have I experienced such an autumn, nor considered anything of the sort possible on earth—a Claude Lorrain projected into the infinite, every day of the same indomitable perfection.

(Nietzsche, 1969, p. 316)

We are forced onto our back foot about the idea of quality in art teaching and learning by Jeremy Bentham's claim that all pleasures are equal. Bentham's remark has the potential to undermine art education and that of Mill's notion of 'higher qualities'.

People have their own personal preferences for why they like a particular kind of art, preferring this art to that art, but Bentham was stating something far more defamatory about any supposed, superior, learner-like attendant higher qualities of art experience in general. For Bentham stated that one pleasure could be as good as another pleasure. So the fact that someone prefers Renaissance art to Minimalist art, on the face of it, demonstrates for Bentham's point that one pleasure is as good as another pleasure.

If I draw an aimless squiggle on a page and can take pleasure from this experience, this pleasurable experience is no better and no worse a pleasurable experience than a visit to Rome to see Michelangelo's paintings in the Sistine Chapel. This contrast highlights why the theory that one pleasure is as good as another pleasure is challengeable. This is not automatically so in art education. In the teaching of art, is one pleasurable experience of an art piece of work and performance just as pleasurable as another piece of art work and performance? I have suggested that in art education, teaching quality and learning differences matter and correspondingly these differences affect our pleasure of an art. By virtue of the art intelligence so presented is usually the way we assess art but this intelligence can be measured in lots of different ways. For welfare maximisation overall to work, higher meaningful art experiences are required which the teaching of art facilitates. Forming aesthetic judgments about art works and performances in education involve the higher qualities of an art for the chief reasons that we want students to develop good habits about art that better serve them and their happiness in the world in ways that are good for them and their communities. If one pleasure is as good as another pleasure, have we demeaned and betrayed the differences that can exist and which would do tremendous damage to our faculty of understanding things in the world related to one's consciousness and comprehension in learner-like ways, the incapacity to realise through cognition, perception, culture and feelings, the strengths, weaknesses and significance of the student's art performance and production?

Mill admired Jeremy Bentham immensely, but did not agree with his claim that all pleasures are equal. Arguably, teachers of art need to be aware of this issue since if all pleasures are equal, the teaching quality of an art need not be concerned about the higher qualities of an art. Because if what only matters is one's own state of pleasure completely content to the exclusion, the denial, the consensus and the understanding that it is the higher qualities of an art that gathers the refinement of its pleasures that all art, past and present, possesses, there cannot be anything rightly commendable about art. In the teaching of art, pleasure and displeasure derives from learner-like grasping of the higher qualities of the art activity that is being taught.

Of course, Bentham could reply to this by saying it is not the highest good in an art practice that he is drawing attention to, but its pleasure. Is he correct in this? Mill held that art education could represent a higher quality of experience and understanding in proportion to the greatest happiness principle that can carry some moral good of the highest interested values of an art. For Mill, art was healthy, or the higher quality of it was. To derive pleasure from absurdity, ridiculousness or from a very offensive piece of work could not be classed as art since they lack the higher qualities of an art seeking intellectual, moral, social, aesthetic and sympathetic human feeling guidance. However, absurdity and ridiculousness fashioned with consciousness and technique representing the higher quality factors in an art can exert beneficial influence, is demonstrated in comedy and comical sketches, which is as ancient as the Greek poets, explored by cartoonists, performers and many novelists and painters, for example.

The critical judgments and appreciative values of an art, the students in an art class cannot ignore and be indifferent about, since if one pleasurable experience is as good as another pleasurable experience, it cancels out much of the higher relevance of art. Bentham might say the higher relevance of an art is still intact but that would be preposterous since the pleasure is conjoined to the higher relevant experience of the art. The pleasure has been stirred by the refinement of the art. Hence the generative circumstances of the pleasurable experience do seem to matter for the cause of the pleasure in art activity in education.

In Mill's essay on Bentham, Mill cites a well know Bentham aphorism that: "quantity of pleasure being equal, push-pin is as good as poetry" (Mill, 1980, p. 95). I have begun to explain what is problematic about this notion. We cannot ignore this because if Bentham is correct, there is a strong case why art education should be at the periphery of an education curriculum, which is what Plato (1997) similarly thought in his *Republic*.

Bentham believed that all pleasures are equal, meaning that one pleasure is as good as another pleasure and that one pleasure in quantity is the same as another pleasure in quantity. In which case the belief is that in ironing my clothes, hanging my clothes out to dry on a washing line and shinning my shoes are pleasures equal to that of poetry. But what does such pleasure restore, what does it furnish and what does it stimulate comparable to that of art activity and its experience? Pleasure is pleasure, is the argument. If push-pin is as good as poetry, the pleasure that a drug addict associates with taking drugs is also equal to poetry. Bentham rules out that the content, cognition, morality, perception and the skill level of an art, for example, may be relevant to the pleasure we experience in the art but no more relevant than the pleasure from push-pin. The quality of the pleasure that is surely occasioned by reading and producing poetry, the student's understanding of a poem which, along with other subsequent poetry readings, enable the student to develop their capacities in proportion to an art task that generally speaking, advances their pleasure of an art.

Therefore, the fact that I can take pleasure from anything and everything is one thing and students in an art class are encouraged to find pleasure from all kinds of objects, performances, skills and experiences. Axiomatically, pleasure can be a random experience but in the teaching of art direction as given, the students profit by the teaching instruction, embracing what they need to consider, understand, determine, reflect upon, produce and achieve accordingly. The students' pleasurable experiences rest upon certain relevant demands of the art, so that while they can take pleasure that has no direct relationship to what the art task demands, the good of the students' pleasure conjoins to the critical judgements of the art task requirements. The informing nature of the art task and the relevance of it for student growth development is why the pleasurable experience of reading poetry and creating it is superior to the pleasure of push-pin and playing it. Push-pin was designed for merriment but the plays of Sophocles and the countless poems one has read and can recall, for example, demand serious reflection of what a certain life can bring to our attention, that redemptively becomes a beneficial experience. The two pleasures are not equal. I can take pleasure from eating toast and drinking tea at breakfast time or any time. Henceforth, if there is no difference between one pleasure and another pleasure, then as Kant construed in *The Critique of Judgment*, pleasure itself is just a matter of free liking (Kant, 1928). We ought also to distinguish that push-pin is a children's game of 16th century origin but art activity and its experiences aren't a game; comparing the pleasure of poetry to push-in cannot logically be a valid comparison. Poetry is much older than push-pin and unlike push-pin which no one really plays any longer, poetry continues. Therefore, if no one is playing the game of push-pin then no one is taking any pleasure from it.

Pleasure *per se*, Kant notes, is "subversive of the judgement of taste" (quality) distorting our approval at the highest level (Kant, 1928, §. 14) of the moral, social and intellectual betterment of what art activity and experience in its refinement can communicate. Bentham is confused about the knowledge, cognition and the performances that a student needs to experience and produce art in order to express the kind of pleasure of an art viewed as healthy, meaningful and relevant in social, intellectual, aesthetic and moral ways. Pleasure does not produce art and this has a substantial bearing in estimating whether push-pin activity and poetry are equal pleasures. So that in the teaching of art the pleasure of art is in proportion to the development of art that makes a contribution to society, of sympathetic shared experiences about life that are not simply private judgments but are particular-universally valid judgments that require a critique and knowledge about its history-tradition.

Kant further indicates that art activity becomes degraded if pleasure as 'free delight', is our estimating faculty of an art. Contrarily, the notion of pleasure may not be there at all in art activity in a self-conscious seeking manner, when the student is concentrating on how to cut, how to sing, how to mould, how to write, how to play this piece of Bach's music. The student may not be consciously aware of any pleasure while playing one of Bach's solo violin pieces but is not unaware of the quality of their art activity and the affectionate stirrings of the music in such moments. They take pleasure from playing the piece well, from the cleverness of the music and from the pleasure they might take from the mood and associated imagery that the music provokes. Furthermore, a student who is learning on the piano to play *The Flea* by Mel Bonis may be concentrating all of his or her intellectual and dexterous efforts on improving their performance of this piece of music. Novelists, poets, musicians, designers, architects, and painters, for example, regard the creation of art as very challenging and difficult. Suppose Bentham returns to say that push-pin requires concentration too then he is opening himself up to the content and action of the activity, the degree of difficulty involved, the effort it requires, its relevant perceptions and cognitions, what is completely comprehended under it and its capital importance morally, socially, intellectual and aesthetically.

To recap, one's pleasurable experience from push-pin expresses an amount of pleasure that is equal to the amount of pleasure from poetry, is Bentham's argument. Presumably the student's pleasure experience from doing a science experiment in a lab is equal to the same pleasure from push-pin too. We experience the same proportions of pleasure because they are equal whether we are eating an ice cream or going to the theatre to watch Shakespeare's *A MidSummer Night's Dream*. But we know this is ludicrous, for however much ice cream I consume over a life time and enjoy it, it has no subject-matter and learner-like higher qualities. Contrarily, if I take pleasure from Shakespeare's *A Midsummer Night's Dream* is it because of what it addresses in life, the fantastical in life, a better way of being in the world, a connection with life, the generous and emotional empathy of life, the beauty of life, what is wrong with life, the difficulty of life, or what is trifling and dull with life, what is insensitive in life, or unpleasurable and exasperating about life?

A theatrical performance of Shakespeare's *A Midsummer Night's Dream* is laden with many moral, intellectual, social, historical, mythological and aesthetic interconnected considerations that my pleasurable experience of the play, however free it is, is still to some extent functionally conditioned by my recognition and understanding of the play's contribution which affects my own imaginative pleasurable reading-experience of the play. That a poem's insight in relation to the life it represents portraying an incident, situation, event and concept, for example, can affect the quality of the pleasure we experience in the poem is naturally subject to our seeing how the incident, situation, event and concept is portrayed, experiencing it for ourselves imaginatively. But in seeing it and experiencing it we are also learning about the powers of how to represent and create meaning and how our pleasure is attached to some extent to the goodness of the representation and the insight of the poem, helping us to understand all manner of things. Our ability to reason would surely demand that we comprehend the poem's understanding in order that our joy from the poem correspondingly produces relevant feelings attributed to the poem. Our delight is then in proportion to the estimating esteem of the poem's art that conditions our judgement of the poem in an alliance of social, moral, intellectual and aesthetic ways. The pleasure is explained and is dependent on the faculty of intelligence, imagination and human sympathetic feelings. It is of necessity, not one of choice, that to a degree we understand the poem in order to experience its delight.

The gratification we take from playing a game of push-pin is allied to winning. While there is an air of seriousness about playing pushpin, a poem's seriousness is one conceptually of tragedy, remorse, regret, love, gaiety, solidarity, friendship, and sympathetic human feelings. What subject content does push-pin have? What human virtues and common human difficulties and failings does it explore? Therefore, the two pleasures are not equal because the higher cognitive quality of poetry demonstrates what push-pin cannot offer because push-pin's pleasure in comparison to poetry is naive. Bentham contrasts two very different kinds of pleasure conceptions. Push-pin's satisfaction is at best a simple satisfactory experience of pleasure. Whereas a poem's satisfaction derives from trained reflections of higher cognitive experiences tied to the poem's relevant representation.

A poem has the advantage of a serious educational reason in light of its powers that are in proportion to its ideas and a strong public sense of the agreed learner-like values of it consisting of discerning thoughts and feelings of penetrative human insight. In admirable and exceptional ways, a poem can be handed down from one generation to another, to experience the beliefs, perceptions and attitudes of life proper for beings living in the world to contemplate. A poem's apprehension of life represents a superior outlook that can be an importantly shared social experience amongst students, typifying existence in keeping with the state of mind in ordinary common life, emancipating and useful for improvement in intellectual, social, moral and aesthetic ways. Thus, to repeat, the quantity of pleasure from push-pin is not of the same magnitude of order conceptually, experientially, imaginatively, feelingly and intellectually as that of poetry.

Bentham's inability to ask himself whether push-pin is capable of contemplating, experiencing and stating what is great and good in the world, shows how little he knew about the results of an art's pleasure that warrants why we might think of the art mentioned as part of the great and good in the world. Which activity: is it push-pin or poetry that stimulates superior cognition or is superior cognition irrelevant to our pleasure? Bare delight can be useful and not useful, but invariably it is small. Is it as G.E. Moore suggests, with Bentham in mind, that "pleasure is pleasure and nothing more than that" (Moore, 1988, p. 12). What stops a poem from being pleasing would be its higher aesthetic, moral, social and intellectual account, but would such criteria and the level of it be a fair way to judge correspondingly push-pin?

The pleasure from a poem may be a painful pleasure due to the intelligent and sympathetic way it might present imaginatively a real struggle and hardship of a life. Kant thought of pleasure as the mere play of sensation in space and time that was, as previously mentioned, not a proper object of a judgement of art. To say to a student that 'this' needs improving in their work, we are talking about the accuracy, value and meaning of the art and the greatness of it making distinctions that don't imply any kind of pleasurable sensations, but rather the inferred standards and capacities of an art. What excites us about art is what pleasurably moves us emotionally and cognitively about the art, involving the aesthetic sense of the object-performance dealing fully and appropriately with its thread of associations and interconnections. Of accomplishments which then assist us in understanding the art and hence what may contribute to our lives, capable of being at the same time valid for everyone according to the conditions, as Kant says, of the judgement that is arrived at.

When an eleven year old is playing the piano, creating a painting, writing a poem, performing in a play or a dance and making a ceramic vase, for example, they are carrying on *ad infinitum* the continuation and evolving nature of art culture in ways push-pin and its pleasure cannot possibly match. Art is a much more severe enterprise and exposition of a judgement, where there is a lot at stake conjoined to the interests and character of the human beings that we are, and where there is an infinite amount of free constructing, evaluating and conveying in art, and that art activity and experience is not like push-pin activity and experience, of playing the same game over-and-over again without much cognitive, imaginative, moral and aesthetic development in it because the magnitude of its pleasure is very simple. For Hegel, a game like push-pin is nothing more than a superfluous form of pleasure compared to art, a light relief, of an activity that at best would be similar to a man who enjoyed throwing lentils accurately through a narrow aperture (Hegel, 1988, p. 44). An art's aesthetic experience and the associated pleasures of it may have been inspired by a nightingale singing, the coping or not of a death in a family and of beauty in the world through kindness affecting, therefore, one's concept of happiness and thus in association one's pleasure in life. Mill believed that art has more justice, more moral feeling, imagination and intellectual conception for helping a human being develop their happiness and live a more refined and fuller existence with social contribution than what push-pin and its pleasure could achieve.

Sometimes in the teaching of art we know it can take some time for the eye, the ear and movement with cognition and imagination working together "to complete the apprehension [of art] from the base to the summit" (Kant, 1928, §.26). The vista, the performance and the account of an art may be all too much to be taken in, in one session due to the art's complexity that can confound us, due to our lack of experience and capabilities and our surprise by what we overlook the more we study the art. The art work is too old, of a culture we are not familiar with and of a 'language' and conceptual idea we have not experienced before. Our human sympathy is too small, our mind insensitive, our prejudice too strong, our spirit faint, our associations lacking ardour, our pleasure unsophisticated, and our engagement dry, whimsical or insipid. We see the art but do not understand and appreciate its greatness; we are whisked away all too easily at times to consider other things. And yet it could be that what "seizes the visitor on entering St. Peter's in Rome. For here a feeling comes home to him of the inadequacy of his imagination for presenting the idea of a whole within that imagination attains its maximum, and, in its fruitless efforts to extend this limit, recoils upon itself, but in so doing succumbs to an emotional delight" (Kant, 1928, §.26). Can the pleasure of push-pin compete with this? Can it attain this elevated kind of pleasure that bestows, as Kant remarks, the same feelings as others would render of the art? Does push-pin posseses this kind of human respect? Does it possess this heightened kind of pleasure that is good for us?

Commonly an arts structure, its story, its music, configuration, idea and its form influences our associated imaginative experiences that retain these things in our free formation experiences of them. We dwell upon the arts sensibility through our own thinking and feeling for the art that produces the kind of reverence possessing a special kind of pleasure from impressions of sense that possesses common human consensual agreement grasping the same art. Obviously students of art are not just taught simply to think, feel, imagine and perceive in an unbounded manner but equally to arrive at judgments through the various measures that the teacher of art will discuss that can apply to the art object, the amount of comprehension and relevance the art has that attracts or repels our higher intellectual, moral, aesthetic and social understanding.

Marcel Duchamp's *Fountain* is not judged by the standards of Van Gogh's *Irises,* the quality of Charlotte Brontë's *Jane Eyre* is not judged by the standards of Frank Kafka's *The Metamorphosis* and the quality of George Handel's *Messiah* is not judged against the standard of George Gershwin's *An American in Paris.* Is this because they are all separated by different traditions of art? It would still be difficult to judge these figures even if they were part of the same movement of art. To compare the quality of art produced by a generation of artists like: James Joyce, George Orwell, D. H. Lawrence, T.S. Elliot, John Steinbeck, Ernest Hemingway, William Faulkner, Katherine Mansfield, and Virgina Woolf for example, begs the question of whether there are many different thoughts, ideas, incidents and relations, truths, untruths, loved and unloved scenes being expressed that our common understanding of their qualities would relate to what we had to say about their individual particular works of art. Kafka is a modernist but the aesthetic quality of his writings intellectually, morally and socially has what all artists have, a uniqueness that cannot be reduced, as Kant remarked, to a set of rules.

While we can say that tragedy and comedy, for example, at such-and-such a time has X quality in it, we still have to experience and perceive the individual, singular and particular way the X quality comes alive, is taken to be, appears spontaneous, is intuitively created, is set against other qualities in the art, is conjoined to them, is defined in this or that character and like no other character, shifts a viewpoint or gives another interpretation of X quality and how it is culturally set. Hence, what we are interested in when we talk about the quality of art in education is how the individual student's work of art has enlarged the student's being in the world in

61

communitarian ways, how the X quality in the student's art work expresses love and unloved experiences that we can imagine and be moved by, how any story a student wrote about in art like learning ways would involve conjointly aesthetic, moral, social and intellectual factors.

The generation gap between one art movement and another art movement may be irrelevant. As the quality of an art can transcend generations of an art so that the drama, the representations, the aesthetic, the intelligence, the morality, the style, the genera, the arrangements and the incidents of it can possess enormous imaginative human value so that we do not think of the art as only of time related significance. "The road opened to the Greek temples and the Gothic cathedrals. I walked towards them feeling the warm touch of the Lascaux painter on my palm" (Herbert, 1985, p. 17). Furthermore, the quality of each writer's body of work and their individual poems, plays, short stories and novels, for example, can be reasonably assessed like any other art for its social, moral, intellectual, aesthetic, economic, practical, creative and sympathetic human feelings. At times, art education may emphasise more autonomy, more convention, more tradition and contemporary work but in a manner that concurs with welfare maximisation overall.

When we talk about the quality of this or that art work, we are usually claiming that the quality of an art involves its features, ideas, concepts, movements and its sympathetic expressed human feelings, for example. "When Ruskin [1877] accused Whistler of flinging a pot of paint in the public's face, he was in effect saying that Whistler could not be putting his paintings [*Nocturne in Black and Gold: The Falling Rock*, c. 1875] forward as candidates for appreciation: he must be engaged in some other cause: and why Ruskin said this was that he could not see what it was in Whistler's paintings that Whistler could possibly be asking us to appreciate" (Wollheim, 1980, p. 165). As brilliant as an art critic John Ruskin was, he was unable to notice how Whistler was indeed a sophisticated painter, whose notion of art and painting was different from his own. Ruskin was being prejudiced. While Whistler's *Nocturne in Black and Gold: The Falling Rock* clearly offended his artistic sensibilities, what seemed to have eluded him was the fact that Whistler was properly trained as a painter in Paris. He admired Velázquez immensely, made copies in the Louvre, was an engraver, was drawn to Japanese art, was a symbolist and was a friend of Courbet, Degas, Monet, Manet, Toulouse-Lautrec and Oscar Wilde and had affinities with the art-for-art's sake movement which in particular Ruskin objected to and Tolstoy also in his book *What is Art* (1994).

Whistler, like many other artists at the time, was more aware of new directions in art expressing libertarian views with ideas about autonomy, abstraction, expressionism, sensuousness, subjectivism, pluralism, eclecticism and experimentation in art. He recognised new ideas feeding into the language of art from those paying attention to essential differences in social existence, moral values, intellectual thinking and art. He had a willingness to see differences in how art and the world was changing, a more varying world with interests in different kinds of art was replacing some of the old values of art by new values of art corresponding to some of the new social inhabitants in our world who were seeing their own significance being more represented in the new art ideas of life. Not before experienced, contributing new likenesses and feelings of life succeeded in opening up more artistic, imaginative contributions from, for example, the notion of art-for-art-sake, that Whistler championed. The art that Whistler painted was clearly not the art that Ruskin nor Tolstoy advocated. In the different qualifications of an art, there are a range of quality issues and these quality issues may have lots of different life associations with being in the world that in a given representation allows for and positively encourages new thinking capable of being communicated. This may be a confirmation of the type of person, music or concept the art is about. The representation is more than likely to have a dynamic all of its own, a confluence, an arrangement, a motif, a life-style expressed, a rhythm, an idea, a concept and emphathy perhaps with its characters; the hummingbird, the mountains, the excited crowd, the reaction, a solid sound, the murmur and the voices of children, women and men.

We are unusually protective of many art productions which enliven us, make us feel more peaceful, humanly sympathetic, disgusted, shameful, grateful, beautiful, in solidarity and moved emotionally by the contingent affects of our own estate of various art productions that we have experienced recounting the art. For example, let us return to St. Peter's Basilica consisting of some of the principal art works of Bramante, Maderno, Bernini and Michelangelo. These art works in St. Peter's Basilica could never be pronounced as high art without common understanding and attachment to these art works. The art displayed readily, intimately and suddenly by association creates the frame of mind in which we are able to grasp the esteem of these art pieces, the mental temperament that comes from our higher facilities of cognition, perception and feeling estimating, in an embodied manner, the amount of intellectual, moral, spiritual and social concerns that such art exhumes. These art works succeed in their rectitude. There is an attraction to this art production because of the humanity communicated by how we can imaginatively experience energetically some of the sculptural human figures in it, for example, advancing ideas about life, discourses, events and human situations as "the mate stands braced in a whaleboat, lanced and harpoon are ready" (Whitman, 1986, p. 37). Is there any comparion between the activity of push-pin and Michelangelo's creation of the facade for St. Peter's Basilica in Rome which, as Jacob Burckhardt mentions, owes its success because Michelangelo satisfied the "universal yearning of the Renaissance by building this grandest and most glorious of giant domes with its light-filled drum" (Burckhardt, 1987, p. 91). Needless to say, will the pleasure of push-pin, as Kant in *The Critique of Judgement* writes, have the same affect upon us as these works of art in St. Peter's Basilica, conferring distinction upon us and our world of what can substantially bring truth home to our feelings, thoughts and imagination? Of revered thoughts and feelings we are not indifferent to because they are part of a higher quality of life which, when cherished, percolate throughout our lives unconsciously and consciously and become evident in subtle ways in our behavior, values and attitudes.

SOCRATES, THE PIG AND THE FOOL

It is as though our society has simply decided that the purpose of schooling is economic – to improve the financial condition of individuals and to advance the prosperity of the nation.

(Noddings, 2005, p. 4)

Mill (2007), in his book *Utilitarianism,* believed that pleasure affects human happiness. Because Mill thought human happiness was essential for a good life, synonymous with the experience of a good life was our associated pleasures of it. But a good life, for Mill, requires certain kinds of pleasures more than others. It was the higher qualities of life, he believed, together with welfare maximization overall policies which facilitate the best human pleasures conducive to the general conditions which are required for construing common standards of interaction and empathy in social life. The higher qualities invoke greater responsible, social thinking, awareness of our freedom, that engages reflective activity with the feelings of pleasure of everyone bearing upon common human action and representations in life. The operations of the higher qualities makes us feel more alive to different points of view in the service of welfare maximization overall supporting, realising, caring for others, assisting, being kind, contributing, cooperating, being generous, exhibiting, displaying, performing, loving, explaining, empowering, imagining, experiencing, criticising, delighting, enjoying and exciting, as part of a life that everyone collectively shares, honors, respects and cultivates. To repeat, the higher qualities of human character and action involve our moral, intellectual, aesthetic, social and human sympathetic feelings.

One of Mill's most famous quotes is: "It is better to be a human being dissatisfied than a pig satisfied; better to be Socrates dissatisfied than a fool satisfied. And if the fool, or the pig, is of a different opinion, it is because they only know their own side of the question. The other party to the comparison knows both sides" (Mill, 2007, p. 8). In the above quote, what Mill is saying, in an imaginative and deliberate starkly presented format, was: who is the better judge of life and who knows both sides of the argument? Is it the pig (completely self-centered and focused on self-gratification), the fool (ignorant and naive) or Socrates (the philosopher)? No contest, because Socrates, out of these three choices, is the only one who has a better understanding of life and is capable of judging both sides of the argument in a social manner. Socrates is cast provocatively and prudently by Mill as the only one of the three figures who possesses enough of the higher qualities of life in relation to the public good, who thus is more capable of taking account of each different position and of advancing utilitarian welfare maximisation overall. The scenario may seem unreal and full of too many unanswered questions, but the message is clear, Socrates is seen as the only person who is sufficiently educated in the higher qualities of life and that is the over whelming point Mill is making.

For good reasons, Mill has clearly decided that it is Socrates who understands better the idea of human happiness and more richly displays it than the pig or the fool. He believes that Socrates leads a worldlier, more flourishing and fulfilling life as the result of being motivated by the higher qualities that in turn benefits welfare maximization overall. Despite the fact that Socrates may be very dissatisfied with his own life due to the circumstances of it, his concept of personal well-being and community well-being conjoined is viewed by Mill to be very different from the pig's and the fool's concept of personal well-being and community well-being. Our pig and our fool, roughly classified, lack the human capacities of a community notion of well-being because neither of them has developed any higher qualities. Children clearly need protecting in law from being preyed upon, but our pig, being self-centered, is oblivious to this and is uninterested in this, while the fool is also oblivious to this and has difficulty understanding it. But such a law would not be sufficient to protect the child if education was not also a legally binding obligation resting on the notion that school life educates children conjoined to the idea of the higher qualities of life. I am interpreting Mill's notion of the fool as someone who has no education at all and the pig as someone who is completely self-centered, un- sympathetic and unwilling to share anything in life. If we all acted like the pig or the fool, the world would not be a better place, is self-evidently a central tenet of Mill's notion of utilitarianism. Many theorists have criticized the generality of Mill's utilitarian thinking with poignant points raised but without recognizing equally the value of it too.

Everyone benefits, as Michael Slote implies, from intellectual, moral, social and aesthetic life even if some benefit from these factors more than others in self-regarding and other-regarding normal, common, virtuous, ethical, overall, broad and in balanced equal weight ways (Slote, 1998). However far fetched the contrast between Socrates, the pig and the fool may be, it resonates, despite criticism by Alasdair MacIntyre of this (2002, p. 227–231).

Mill's contention was that a pig and a fool, in different ways and owing to their respective imagined but perceivable and likely character flaws, will display: obstructive, greedy, uncaring, ignorant, uncooperative, narrow, helpless, prejudicial, unneighbourily, vulnerable, unthinking, gullible, afraid, unhappy and unpleasant behavior and that, therefore, their ideas of human happiness would be skewed. Neither of them is sufficiently capable of promoting the feeling of moral, intellectual, social and aesthetic understanding that, therefore, is necessary for happiness in life to thrive that takes account of welfare maximization overall. The pig is too greedy and the fool is uneducated. So, a further point about Mill's Socrates is that he recognises that the pig wants more and the fool needs care in the community and an education. If our fool gets care in the community and an education his quality of life is improved. If our pig is willing to share then his quality of life is also improved. Utilitarianism, as Slote mentions, is self-regarding and other-regarding in a normal, common, virtuous, ethical, overall manner. Hence self-centeredness and unthinking reflective views of pleasure are not what constitute social happiness in life. Arising from such conditions are nothing more than frivolous and dangerous notions of human happiness and pleasure in life, exerting no relation to the higher quality mental powers and actions needed in common for the public good.

I have indicated that Mill appreciated art education for reasons to do with the public good and our pleasures in life. In his autobiography he mentions that art experience was a cardinal point in his ethical and philosophical thinking. Too many theorists have ignored this point. Why did Mill think this? For Mill, the value of art education as a higher quality is how it confirms and enlarges our being in world. He believed that art production is capable of estimating, reflecting and informing our common notions of human happiness and pleasure in the world expressing the higher qualities of life befitting the manifestation of our understanding of the world and adding to it. To dismiss art education as trivial would be to undermine how Mill felt about the happiness principle since art aesthetic education is one of the instruments expressing the experiences, actions and contemplations that brings into our lives noble feelings; that art appreciation in shared ways is a splendid thing when containing venerable ideas, thoughts and feelings about life imbued with living. Mill's point is that our pig and our fool could benefit from an art aesthetic education.

Drawing upon his own experience, Mill asserted in his autobiography that art education presents fresh insights that enter into the play of our learner-like attachments, for poetry, literature, music, sculpture and painting, for example, were capable of strengthening and bringing into view our conceptions of an art and our feelings for it. Reading poetry and literature, for example, Mill discovered delights relating to the nature of the art which he had never experienced before; an inward joy and sympathetic imaginative experiences, which he surmises could be shared by all human beings. Art represented a different power of mind for him for visualing, feeling, conceptualising, understanding and experiencing life resting upon more subjective rather than objective judgements. Declaring that art has value that can affect the formation of our human character by opening up, freeing and expanding our consciousness in unexpected ways, promoting the real qualities of things, ideas, incidents and events intelligible and satisfying. The beneficial feelings from art (aesthetic experience), Mill suggests, could motivate the creation of new thoughts, deepen human sensitivity, inject freshness, quickness, a greater love of life, independent conclusions and community solidarity in the world; an outpouring in spontaneity of unusual and intense thinking and imagining which productively could intersect an idea-feeling leading to new discoveries and solutions, as shown, for example, in the work of Leonardo da Vinci, Mozart, Shakespeare and Picasso. But it should not go amiss that in our ordinary common lives, art experience has application and trajectory too, just as assuredly of the kind of real joy Mill experienced, that equally in an infinite variety of ways when comprehending such art, its production stimulates our imagination, helping conjointly our human intelligence and happiness in the world. The fact that a poem or a painting, Mill argued, could express our associated, "intense feeling of the beauty of a cloud lighted by the setting sun" (Mill, 2008, p. 84) is no erroneous or delusional object of experience and neither does it hinder nor undermine, he maintained, an analysis of the cloud in a scientific way.

Mill implied that if human happiness was subject to impulse only as our feelings of pleasure and displeasure, we would clearly lack the higher qualities of life which more commonly and sensibly aid our human happiness in the world. Thus a despotic state of being in the world is not paying any regard to human happiness because it does not have the capacity of an excellence capable of weaving into its thought knowledge, determination and understanding. The only way to live a happy and pleasurable life, Mill believed, related to the higher qualities of life represented by: intellectual, moral, social, human sympathetic feelings and aesthetic higher thoughts in imaginative ways. Therefore, an educational system where students are, in learner-like ways, developing higher qualities of life would reciprocally have recourse to pleasures more meaningful and enriching for common human happiness. The higher qualities of life facilitates welfare maximization overall policies and vice versa evincing us of the acts that best serve human happiness personally and in community human flourishing ways for everyone. Mill was of the view that intellectual, moral, social and aesthetic higher experiences are beneficial to human beings because properties of understanding, feeling and reasoning capable of expressing moral, social and aesthetic higher order representations of life in productions, performances and in the readings of art, in learner-like ways, form the basis of consensual claims of agreement that are seen as relevant to human flourishing. While the pig thinks differently and the fool is uneducated, life for them fails to attain models of cultural life that inculcates, as Mill suggests, what furthers our human happiness. The aesthetically refined higher standards of cultural life begin and are fully present in young children's drawings of squares and in their paintings of circles, a star in the night sky, a snow flake and their use of the colour purple for a purpose that assuredly adds verve and meaning to their art work.

Our pig and fool may seem like hedonists because they are consumed on the face of it by their own pleasures, but their pleasures are misguided. A utilitarian teaching response would be that our pleasures don't restore being in the world, 'if we are ignorant of what makes life go well for people, then you will be unable to make your own life or the lives of others go well" (Crisp, 1997, p. 20). Therefore, the pig and the fool, as Mill portrays them, are affected by forces independent of an education. Our pig is represented as a force consumed by its self-gratification which makes it unhealthy in intellectual, moral, social and aesthetic refined ways, while our fool is represented as irrational, helpless, stupid and vulnerable making him unhealthy intellectually, morally, socially and aesthetically in refined ways. Neither of them possess any sufficient higher quality experience of life as a source of joyfulness for them in the form of an awakening, a restoration or social bonding involving decisions about their pleasures and human happiness in community consensual ways.

For Mill, the higher faculties being moral, intellectual, social and aesthetic, dwarf that of the pig's or the fool's intelligence in ways they cannot consistently, if at all, keep in view. So one point about welfare maximisation overall in education with emphasis on the development of the higher faculties, is for students to achieve, understand and cooperate keeping in view a social life retaining substantial human sympathetic feelings serving our wellbeing and our human flourishing in publically good ways.

Mill asserts that the higher faculties also help society to resolve their conflicts of interest to form a concord of social views of life that are beneficial to all people. While the higher faculties duly contemplated are what can lead many of us out of our problems, Mill also suggests that the very presence-activity of the higher faculties in shown mimetic ways undermines the pig's and the fool's interests. It is life's higher cultural, social and democratic life that, Mill asserts, enables us to lay down our superior concerns for life. Mill, like Kant and Hegel, believed that culture is a requisite for the judgement of art with moral feeling. An untutored moral, intellectual, aesthetic and social person, Kant thought, could be terrifying if let loose on a world where there are many vices and dangers. Socrates, Mill intimates, shows his love for the world, but the pig and the fool cannot do this or cannot do this sufficiently because the pig is self-centred and the fool lacks understanding of the issues necessary to make informed decisions. Life becomes bent out of shape and society falls apart, Mill implies, without continual preparation and training, instruction and experience, and discussion and dialogue in the higher pleasures of life for all of us proportionately, of the concerns that relate to welfare maximisation overall.

However general this discussion certainly seems, it does lead appropriately back once again into an educational art focused approach concerning the qualities of art in teaching and learning. There are further learner-like situations of special concern for the teacher of art, when the student feels frustration with how their art work is progressing. For example, when a student has to rework a drawing or has to go over again and again their dance routine only to feel still dissatisfied with the art results they have produced. These experiences can contribute to making the art work either worthwhile or un-worthwhile for them. Finding the acting troublesome, the model-making troublesome, the fabric troublesome, the playing of the clarinet troublesome, the camera angle troublesome and the idea we thought was good but is now troublesome. It might be that the quality of consciousness the students need to realise for themselves, with the help of the teacher pointing out what is unresolved, in order to distinguish what is capable of being resolved.

The continuing increase of the pursuit of quality in developmental ways in art by the student will sometimes have to involve reimagining other solutions, taking a different course of action in a reforming manner that then produces the required higher qualities of an art. Our students' frustrations with their art work induce a repellant-uneasy feeling that corresponds to a violent temper of mind. This can be the right kind of consonant unease under given circumstances, that in turn provokes the students' own critical faculties out of which suddenly in the woven fabric, the playing, the dance and the camera angle, for example, our student sees something different producing a new comprehension that then advances their art. However, a student also might find their art task too much of a burden. That the art task is asking too much of them too quickly. The savoir-faire of the task may be asking too much of their capabilities. Consequently they may lose confidence in themselves which in turn prevents them from being stimulated by higher art qualities because they cannot recognise them. If the student is unable to recognise the higher qualities of art, it is obviously important that the art teacher attempts to get to the root of the student's problem. This might mean helping the student recollect previous experiences involving common features and ideas which then lead to further discussion with showing and explaining. These methods enable the student to feel refreshed and re-acquainted about how to achieve a range of contrasts and similarities so that the student is able to imitate in order to illuminate from other art examples and from other students' art work in their own imaginative ways addressing the kind of qualities the art exercise required.

We can be sad rather than delighted, or sad and delighted, or frustrated and disappointed, or feel pleased when perhaps we should feel a little vexed by the finished result of the art we have produced. A seam of a dress, a few lines of a poem, a few musical notes can cause us to feel positive and negative (where the negative could be a positive too), so that the experience alters our convictions about the art work and the students' conceptions of the art they have produced. In the teaching of art there are going to be moments when students can learn to love teaching criticism of their art work provided the criticism is not belittling and undermining and it is timely, relevant, constrained, required, and the student can understand its reasons. Not a lot of art in learner-like practice progresses without: 'see if you can play it more like this", 'can we go over this scene of the play again, because this time when you sit down on the sofa on the stage I want you show that you are much more relaxed in this environment, so that the audience know by this relaxing attitude of yours how you fit into this play', 'I like the way you have shaded this as it really gives the figure three-dimensionality but here the shading in this area is not good partly because the structure of the form is not right, the proportions are wrong. Can you see this as I point to the model and as I measure it? Can you see what I see now; how the fingers are more bent at the knuckles than you have them in your drawing. Now look at my thumb nail sketch I have drawn for you here.'.

What could our pig and fool gain from these experiences? Welfare maximization overall is operating in these encounters which holds out the prospect that our pig and our fool could be educated. An education that in one sense is capable of measuring student progress in art education interrelatedly involving students' capabilities, identities, comprehension of subject matter and task-activity standards. A curriculum of art exploring progressive apprehensions of art, culture and life, of material so presented to the student class that in delightful and stretching ways it explores, investigates and produces through art ideas involving understanding, cognition, reason, imagination, perception, feeling and skills grasping progressively and competently higher sympathetic common feelings of life.

Mill is correct about the importance of pleasure in peoples' lives, but to reiterate, this was not the pleasure of the pig or the fool that he had in mind. In an art educational lesson, pleasure is commensurate to the art educational learning task. Our pig's and fool's vulgar, timorous or pathetic sense of pleasure in a progressive teaching way would be subject to alterations, comparisons, recognitions and questions enabling the pig and the fool to see the providence and delights from the higher pleasures of art. The quality of the student's art being an estimate of their pleasure forming experience of the art task that in learner-like ways through the teaching of art is subject to the student being able to grasp the requirements of the art task. The pleasure experience is confined to the attendant bounds of the art task and that further, within these bounds, student pleasure is derived from their consciousness of the art's animated ideas, conceptions, perceptions and actions. Students' pleasurable experiences subsequently undergo changes due to different measurements, revelations and revisions as the art teacher discusses, explains and shows to the students further appreciative aspects of the art to be considered, so moving the art production forward.

Learning requires a sense of pleasure taken from the activities of an art and the student's experience of it. This begins, perhaps, by retaining some of the delight, however small, from our previous experiences and achievements in art education. Taking pleasure from previous experiences that have involved using planes, saws, chisels, machinery, paintbrushes, cameras, sewing machines, musical instruments, word plays, dancing and acting scenes, for example, and in the process knowing a little about what these things can do, can appear like solid, remembered moments of pleasure that continually and unconsciously remain with us expressing what art production can feel like.

If we do not take pleasure from the art activity in the associated ways I have been explaining, the experience of an art lesson task would conceal, for example, its delicate sculpture lines, related to ideas, from us. There would be no trumpet playing in the world if the trumpet music playing did not move us with the feeling it aroused in us in sympathy with it. We might never adopt, rearrange, adjust, develop and reinvent the stability, continuity and the changes in our environment and of being in the world that art activity can provoke if no felt-cognitive pleasure materialised. Was Ruskin right when he said: "it is the child's spirit, which we are mostly happy when we most recover; remaining wiser than children in our gratitude that we can still be pleased with a fair colour, or a dancing light" (Ruskin, 1960, p. 38)? In a teaching manner would we further agree with Ruskin that art has two virtues, "first, the signs of our own good work; secondly, the expression of our delight in better work than our own" (Ruskin, 1960, p. 37)? A teacher tells one of their piano students 'well done that was great' but, later in same the year the whole musical class goes to listen to a piano concerto by Mozart. The students listening at this point could quite possibly feel overwhelmed and inspired from this performance. A group of students in an art class produced a range of abstract paintings which the art teacher praises for being exciting, imaginative, colourful, dramatic, movement and shape coordinated work. Later in the same year the same students go to see a major exhibition of American Abstract Expressionist painters consisting of Adolph Gottlieb, Mark Rothko, Jackson Pollock, Robert Motherwell, Willem de Kooning and others and reported afterwards to their art teacher that they were knocked out by the work they saw. A boy's sister who is sixteen years old reads a short-story she has written to her 10 year old brother about a brother-sister friendship. As the last lines to the story finish, her younger brother gives her a tight hug, remarking how he wished he could write as well as his sister. It is not only in professional art work that students can find delight in better work than their own but in many other guises.

Praise, development and reassurance promote the idea of pleasure in learning, the notion that the students are doing a good job. A pleasurable experience is one of the human forces that we all positively respond to; who doesn't like being told they are doing a great job? Praise, therefore, can be a principle of continuity and change in the student work that stimulates them to do even better. It makes them feel good about themselves. All praise is very much part of the continuity of teaching that gives the student further confidence. Excellence relates to capability in education. Dewey remarked that "lack of understanding of human nature is the primary cause of disregard for it" (Dewey, 1974, p. 63).

In the interest of individual students and whole class teaching, to offer thanks, 'well done everyone', 'this is great', 'this is very interesting' 'that is delightful', and 'I like your idea', are examples that the teacher cares and values students' contributions. These are statements that represent signs that the art work is advancing. If a student was never told, or seldom told, that they are doing good work would this student's confidence, enthusiasm, satisfaction, cooperation and learning focus suffer?

A teaching environment has to be outwardly generous and benevolent to students because it produces, as stated, more positive learning results. Our feelings of pleasure also connect in learner-like situations, as Kant remarked, in a way echoed by Mill and as stated previously, that pleasure can be in conjunction with our understanding with a view to cognition by means of the imagination (Kant, 1928, §. 1), operating at the level of our capability and experience in life. But there would be much that could stand in the way of this kind of experience, if the student is not listened to, if they are not encouraged to speak candidly what is on their own minds and if they are not seen as a fellow equal in class, respected and engaged. 'Who needs me', 'who befriends me', 'who shares things with me' and 'am I a stranger in this class' all affects the student's ability to feel pleasure with cognition and imagination. All students need to feel a sense of success regularly and equally distributed in the class, conjoined, inevitably, to issues of how to improve their art work. We can short circuit a student's sense of pleasure related to their social life and their 'understanding with a view to cognition by means of the imagination' when, for example, in an art activity they are prevented from exploring, inventing, admiring, cooperating, agreeing, challenging and experimenting. Our pig and our fool must be given the means that will enable them to leave behind their misconceptions which can only come by them being willing to seriously entertain through teaching facilitation, filling them with appropriate tasks that gradually and by degree relative to their capabilities make them progress due to what stirred their delight of an art's higher qualities in activity, a recognition that contributes to their conscious good public life.

ARE WE TEACHING HIGH ART OR LOW ART?

We are apt to call barbarous whatever departs widely from our own tatse and apprehension; but some find the epithet of reproach retorted on us.

(Hume, 1965, p. 3)

References to high-art notions span the globe. Centuries of continuous and changing conceptions of high art have involved, for example: ideas about the grand and the common, the technical study of its rhetoric concerns, its indifferent morality or lack of any firm moral basis to it, its notions of beauty, perfectionism, emotion, idealism, formalism, the sublime, taste, academic painting and correctness, can be found in the work of Homer, Aeschylus, Aristophanes, Sophocles, Plato, Aristotle, Longinus, Joshua Reynolds, David Hume and Clive Bell. So consequently, we are sometimes asked in art education whether the art we are teaching is: 'high art' rather than 'low art', 'high culture rather than low culture', 'high art rather than popular art', 'high art rather than student-centered art'. What are all these different distinctions with 'high' and 'low' in them segregating? What are their contrasts? Can we segregate what we teach in art in these ways and ought we to do so?

'High art' is poor art if, as Marcel Proust satirically mocks, we confuse art with 'high society', 'social ambition' and 'special friendships in the art world' (Proust, 2001, p. 59–67). Proust was aware that in the history of art no continent, nation and single group of people have a monopoly over what is 'high art'. The above terms with 'high' and 'low' in them certainly imply a clash of ideas about teaching in art, but if so, why should popular teenage music necessarily clash with classical instrumental music, since on the one hand classical music can perform in instrumental ways Beatles songs rather well, and popular music can have instrumental orchestral influences that can benefit its music interest. A teenager can like popular hip-hop music, jazz, soul, rock and blues and at the same time equally enjoy Mozart concertos and symphonies. Should we discourage students from liking a whole range of musical tastes in art?

From some of Giambattista Vico and Johann Gottfried Herder's thinking, Isiah Berlin explains (Berlin, 1998) that art throughout its history has produced populist, expressionist and pluralist movements of art mutually attached, self-realising and reinforced by the social common life of different communities. All manner of different voices, accents, sentiments, melodies, roughness, coarseness, delicateness and elegance has been part of art expression, stress, volume, ideas and metaphors. Aristotle wrote an important work about rhetoric that clearly is not the language used by poets, musicians and painters for example, who will often arrange their work so that it expresses the quality and imagination of a humanising experience. The art of poetry, for instance, uses particular words to communicate individual experiences of life as evidence of a relative truth. It does so often with sympathetic insight of how human beings may see each other, imaginatively revealing their intimate thoughts, attitudes and ignorance with emotional evocation. The poet Stephen Spender writes:

> My parents kept me from children who were rough
> Who threw words like stones and wore torn clothes
> Their thighs showed through rags they ran in the street
> And climbed cliffs and stripped by the country streams.

(Spender, 2000, p. 134)

"Poetry is an aural art like music" (Arbuthnot, 1959, p. 4) and is usually full of sensitive, sensory human images, a cocophany of literary, rhythmic and clashing sounding words, emotional embodiment, a physical, concrete and imaginative sense experience of being in the world, with verses, similies and metaphors, for example. Stephen Spenders' poem is typical of such art and is a poem expressing a reaction against disenfranchisment, dehumanising experiences and brutality in the world. The temper of this poem is not designed to be academically clever, smug, logical or high-minded. Rather in a poetic, imaginative manner what it is signifying instead is how an insensitive Machiavellian human mind, possessed of a skewed superority of itself, can dismissively and gratituitously reject other human beings. Art is a way whereby we can understand our world and ourselves better but it does not do as the above poem indicates by insisting on objective language, nor necessarily insisting on cosmopolitan, bourgeois or avant-garde notions of art, because in the teaching of art we can can just as fruitfully turn to primitive common utterances, which as Berlin mentions, is not the literal speech of humans but the imaginative, subtle and sophisticated speech of humans expressing metaphoric significance. For example: "blood boiling within him...the teeth of ploughs, the mouths of river, or the lips of vases...with necks and tongues, metals and minerals with veins, the earth had bowels, oaks had hearts, skies smiled and frowned, winds raged" (Berlin, 1998, p. 344). Plato, we know, objected strongly to the use of poetic language, but students can learn how to recognise, recapture, attribute and alter the character of a person and express a landscape, feeling or object that in associative ways has involved us thinking differently, imaginatively and senuously that is an important notion of social growth (Berlin, 1998, p. 360). Plato's way of thinking could never replace, for example, the quality satisfaction we justly feel of the sense of human comfort, joy and meaning that Herbert conveys when he visits the Greek Doric temple in Paestum: "the sky is bronze. The golden chariot of Helios rolls down to the sea. For Homer 'all paths darken'" (Herbert, 1985, p. 29).

The word 'like' causes purists, fans, theorists and die hard followers of an art to cringe at the mention that 'I like their art'. But the word 'like' is a term of endearment. Experts on Mozart, Wagner, Titian, Goya, Austen, Blake and Milton, for example, may find it difficult to accept anything other than 'wonderful' and 'marvelous', as a substitute for the lesser meaningful expression that 'I like these images by Goya' (his *Caprichos* series of etchings 1796–77). Of course, Goya is a wonderful and fantastic artist. Yet 'like' has its uses because to say 'this art exercise was pleasant', 'I am pleased with this', 'that it was agreeable', 'this was satisfying', 'I have a fondness for flowers' and 'I like this' all such phrases can capture a person's ordinary and proper aesthetic outlook. Having a fondness for flowers, for example, may just be the insight that the teacher of art may need, knowing that flowers motivate a particular student.

In context, for a student to remark that they 'like it', is not an unusual kind of response to make having heard the particular aesthetic quality of the music, to find that it invokes in the student a sense of their enjoyment. It is an understandable conviction to make, given that this music and their response to the music is a reasonable, associated judgment to make since music often provokes the feeling of excitement. 'I like this music' becomes a projection of how the student feels about the music that in discussion is representative of their experience of the music. At the same time a young student may see a Goya painting and declare to their teacher that it is a wonderful painting. An expert in art might reasonably claim that such a young student does not know enough about 'this' painting and its significance in the field of art in general, to make such a distinction. However, there is no denying that this is how the young student feels and while they are certainly not as clever as an expert in art, what they have said about the art work is not an unusual response to art of this magnitude. Feeling emotionally overpowered or overcome by the art has already perhaps enlarged the student's appreciation of the art.

'I like this' used in a different situation or too often applied without further reflection may show unwillingness on our part, an inability to further discriminate. A student may have difficulty understanding their art work due to a lack of aesthetically expressed experiences, imagination and reasoning conjoined to their inability or unwillingess to perceive the strong qualities and features of an art. In addition, they may have difficulty seeing 'this as a that' and if they have no conceptually based idea that is used to arouse them in the production of their art, nothing strikes them motivationally to enable them. A lot of difficulties in teaching art may have come about because the students may never have seen a Goya painting and discussed it, read a poem by Blake, listened to Wagner or read a novel by Jane Austen or Margaret Atwood, for example. A student's appreciation for art, therefore, becomes limited. On first view the artists just mentioned may not seem important, but they might, in a cold, indifferent, destructive, dehumanised world detaching itself of the sensibilities of art, prepare us to love something as Kant remarks (Kant, 1928, §. 29) and as Zbigniew Herbert in *Barbarian in the Garden* (1985), Martha Nussbaum (1990) in *Love's Knowledge* and as Iris Murdoch (1993) in *Metaphysics as a Guide to Morals* also highlight. To cherish people's lives and to produces those references-representations which are capable of corresponding to them, to become more aware of other cultures, doing good in the world because an art has taught us how to look and hear as well as being a consoling experience, that in addition helps us to feel more invigorated in common ways, that "art gives a clear sense to many ideas which seem more puzzling when we meet with them elsewhere and it is a clue to what happens elsewhere" (Murdoch, 1997, p. 106).

Young children, conscious of their own aesthetic experiences, admiringly find certain things 'pretty' whose display is enriching to them without necessarily knowing why. What they see as 'pretty' gives life to their being in the world, where seeing 'pretty things' can be justified by common agreement that the object is pretty.

"'So you would carpet your room—or your husband's room, if you were a grown woman, and had a husband—with representations of flowers, would you?' said the gentleman. 'Why would you?' 'If you please, Sir, I am very fond of flowers,' returned the girl.

'And is that why you would put tables and chairs upon them, and have people walking over them with heavy boots?'

'It wouldn't hurt them, Sir. They wouldn't crush and wither, if you please, Sir. They would be the pictures of what was very pretty and pleasant, and I would fancy—

"Ay, ay, ay! But you mustn't fancy', cried the gentleman, quite elated by coming so happily to his point'" (Charles Dickens, 1989, p. 8).

If the expression 'I like this' is not a legitimate and reasonable response to make when listening to the music of Sibelius, that flowers are pretty or this chair my grandad has is nice, then one has not really understood art. Like is part of the state of being evinced by an art. The word 'like' comes easy to a child and is readily used by them in ways that can appear indiscriminate but is not necessarily an inconsistent or inappropriate response to art. How much of a fulfilling life would we all have if we were unable to grasp and treasure a warm welcome, a simple act of kindness, a smile, or mosses and lichens? Suddenly, having appreciated these rudimentary and perhaps vital expressions and occurrences, we are now open to liking many more things and need to do so if we are to have a fulfilling life.

Of course, what a student likes about an art maybe isn't sophisticated, but in their recollections about "Harry Potter', 'Tom Thumb', 'Sleeping Beauty', "Huckleberry Finn', "Little Women', 'The Arabian Nights', The "Diary of a Wimpy Kid' and 'I like dancing', 'playing the piano', 'painting', 'fishing' and 'I like working with fabrics', are the students' overflowing, passionate experiences forming a construction and image whose state has been conditioned by a cause, representing an ideality that will encourage a student to read another book, compose another poem, paint another painting, produce another garment, advance their musical understanding. 'Mr Smith, I like this painting' represents a judgement caught up in the properties and character of the painting that has formed an invisible part of what strengthens the student's intellect and has captivated their imagination to such a degree that the student will then strive, with the help of the art teacher, to study more diligently, produce and improve, with greater accomplishment, their art understanding.

We might assert that there is no clash between 'high art' and 'low art' but that would be a disingenuous statement since the terms in the opening paragraph of this chapter imply definite differences and that these differences of 'high' and low' art matter in the teaching of art. This means that there are different qualities of an art and different conceptions of an art, related to values that affect the art being implied here with different standards of art in mind and those different qualities and standards of art in mind represent 'high art' and 'low art' teaching instruction and attained learner-like understanding.

If we intend to use the terms 'high art' and 'low art' we ought to remember that these terms are riddled with problems: what do we mean by 'high art' and 'low art', and how can we tell the difference, especially if I happen to believe that 'decorative art' is representative of 'low art'. We seem to have forgotten that a great deal of decorative art continues to affect many forms of art, the higher quality of it corresponding to a highly prized commodity in society. A student interested in decorative art will progressively get to know a great deal of decorative art history, will be trained to think creatively, with different forms of representation and degrees of abstraction, in ideas and concepts, techniques-skills that impose a certain decorative pattern to the art. In valuing decorative art we are deriving maybe what will move us to create. A precise art's pattern exploring a side of the student's consciousness might put down on paper for example, in appearance, forms that have a resemblance to nature, human form, geometry, illusion, surrealism, cubism and romanticism. Perhaps the decorative design shows a lot of interpreted movement in appearance and contrasting textures. Perhaps it has a profusion of colours and tones, a sense of space, volume and lustre, rhythm and unity or disunity in the decorative design. A decorative pattern arouses our associative-imaginative human sympathetic feelings of life that we see presented in for example, sculpture, wood carving, stone work, a painting, a ceramic bowl and in textile printed fabrics or wallpaper. Of subjects and impressions recollected and narrated, symbolizing spontaneous and graphic, a sensuous spiritual production of art that has produced upon the mind what can make it valuable, desirable and enable it to be part of a specific social identity confirming culture of a society, resisting the notion that 'decorative art' is then 'low art'.

So while it may be true that Aboriginal, African, Arabesque, Islamic, Art Nouveau, Art Deco, Gothic, the Arts and Craft movement, Eugéne Delacroix, Gustav Klint and Henri Matisse, within their own spheres of art and purposes, produced creative decorative motifs-objects, we can love by intuition, reason, imagination, instinct and feeling, the intentional constructive nature of a decorative art that continues to be adapted to cultural iconography, random details of the world, precious visions and our sense of belonging. Thus the decorative can be culturally and notationally defined. Every time we feel tempted to give an example of 'high art' or 'low art' a counter example might also be given to rebuke our examples. How far can we stretch the notion of high art or low art and still maintain that there is integrity in the way we categorise art production assumingly as high or low?

If we were to mention Egyptian art, Byzantine art, Greek art, Benin Art, Baroque art, Renaissance art, Romantic art, Maori art, Impressionism, Fauvism, abstract art, portrait art, Pop art, Dadaism, Surrealism, Cubism and so on, what do they all have in common and would we describe them all as 'high art'? Is 'high art' then synonymous with art movements? Most definitely but what does Greek art and Gothic art have in common as 'high art'? Do cultures decide what high art is? Most definitely, but neither Greek nor Gothic art thought about art in the same way. Since we live in a pluralistic society, high art is not one cultural practice but many cultural practices. If we say it is the institutional culture of art that determines the above art movements as 'high art', then, what is the institutional culture of art today? All of the above art movements are definitely sophisticated art movements but the institutional culture of art today would further include: feminist art, political art, documentary art, performance art, film art, animation art, public art, Puerto Rican art, African American art, the Prairie school of art, further avant-garde notions of art, community centre art activities, graphic art and rap art. So given such a diverse range of art practices can we still maintain within the teaching of art that students learn about 'high art' and 'low art' practices?

Of course there are inferior works of art all around us, from the past and present: uncultured, manipulative, obscene, vapid, trite, insipid, dull, banal, mean, cheap, vain, demeaning, elitist, pompous, disrespectful, objectionable and cruel. Low-level cobbled together ideas, performances, objects and environments in the above described ways do not inspire anyone, generating instead problematic configurations of art and the social world. Therefore, art that is perceived to have poor visual-performance quality to it, art that is lacking sufficient conceptual discrimination and art that offers nothing spiritually lifting for the human soul, art that is not felt as awe inspiring, an art that has no 'aura' to it (Leddy, 2001, 207), that is not exhilarating, knowledgeable or moving, an art without a distinctive, warm impression of character or place, offer least support and desensitises being in the world. Good art teaching sensitises being in the world in ways bearing on external creations and internal thoughts and feelings conjoined that I have previously expounded; cherishing life, objects and the environment in ways that assist the employment of reason and understanding related to specific insights and experiences that we are short of and in need of in education, but too often fail to notice or sufficiently care to advance.

To decide if an art production is crass, we would judge this on an individual basis, having seen, listened to and read the particular art piece against a range of criteria relevant insights. To point out emphatically the obvious by now, art in education does not teach art from a position of crass and demeaning conceptions of art and life. Because crass and demeaning conceptions do not advance any of the qualities of an art that are tied to the needs of society as values of welfare maximisation overall: intellectually, socially, morally and aesthetically in an alliance that are the high quality values transfigured by art history and the current practice of art.

Classical instrumental music is rightly considered as 'high art'. Yet, classical instrumental music has always been drawn to fairly tales, folkloric fantasy, monsters, trolls, elves and ghouls for inspiration. What major ballet company has not performed various versions of Tchaikovsky's *The Nutcracker Suite, Swan Lake* and *Sleeping Beauty* as well as, Prokofiev's *Cinderella* and *Peter and the Wolf*? Edvard Grieg's *Peer Gynt* is based on Henrik Isben's play and Isben, in turn, loved Norwegian folk art stories while not forgetting Richard Wagner's *The Ring Cycle*. The fairy tales and folk art stories of Hans Christian Andersen, the Brothers Grimm, Greek, Roman, Icelandic, German, African, Aboriginal, Indian, Chinese and Arabic creations are generally considered to be aesthetically rich in associative, allegorical, moral, philosophical, larger than life figures, messages and wonders that have informed generations of people and communities about aspects of art and life. While monsters, trolls, fairies, dragons, giants and elves are figments of our imaginations, have folkloric traditions of art made countries richer or poorer because of such creations? Consequently, it would be fair to say that when a five year old is reading the story *Cinderella* or a thirteen year old is reading J.R. Tolkien's *Lord of the Rings*, that they are being captivated by the very material of a culture of high art, as representatively different paradigm cases of an art. Imagination is a hallmark of art. In different ways too, Nick Hornby's *Fever Pitch,* Marilyn French's *The Women's Room and* Cormac McCarthy's *The Road* and the Beatles music are all cultural cases of high art.

A teacher will admire a child in their class who, for the first time, has learnt to add simple numbers together or has painted their first painting in an art class, partly because they will know that the higher pleasures of an art always retain their simple pleasures of an art. However great a mathematician or painter may be, they retain their appreciation of the simple pleasures of their art and its wonder. The simple pleasures of an art are not only a necessary condition for pursuing higher pleasures of an art but for retaining the art's vital cultivation for sustaining an inquisitive, developing student enquiring mind. The student's inculcation of the simple pleasures of an art which they have learnt in school, are not the superficial qualities of an art. There is an awful lot of perceptual, conceptual, performance, physical and aesthetic, cognitive, creative problem solving involved when learning to sing a nursery rhyme in tune for the first time in a school's choir.

We might then come to the conclusion that 'high art and 'low art' are very inappropriate terms for art educational purposes. Both terms are an injustice to art, a negation of the aesthetic life of art because we can appreciate art in many diverse different ways. There is beauty in Dante's *Divine Comedy* and there is beauty in a seven year old's painting of their mum and dad. What have we here? A seven year old's painting of his mum and dad can hardly be comparable to Rembrandt's 1642 painting *Night Watch,* or any other of his paintings or any painting by a professional artist. But a seven year old's painting of his mum and dad does not have to be comparable to a Rembrandt and in case we temporarily have forgotten, a seven year old would not understand the comparison and appreciate sensitively how Rembrandt uses oil paint to convey emotion and heighten drama in his paintings, for example. The beauty of a seven year old's world as they experience it in education is what can motivate them spontaneously and reflectively in intellectual, moral, social and aesthetical ways for a sought-for expression of a snap-shot image of their world. This seven year old student's world and how they see beauty in it, is the basis that projects a seven year old's painting of their mum and dad.

One of the first things an educationalist might ask is whether this seven year old's painting exercise qualifies as an art task? The painting exercise is part of an art curriculum. An account of it educationally, culturally, and institutionally gives it validity. Equally, this is a 'painting exercise in art' which makes it a proper classifying case of art. In addition, this painting exercise is an example of a continuous practice of art in education with a "highly sensitive historical context for generating-constructing art" (Levinson, 1996, p. 153) that the teacher of art can draw upon and is aware of. This further reinforces the idea that this is an art exercise with legitimacy.

Assuming we accept that this painting exercise is an art exercise and the evidence appears irrefutable, it still does not answer the question whether a seven old's painting of his mum and dad can be seen as a 'beautiful painting'? This would educationally depend on whether we think there is artistic value in this art exercise continuous with art history, culture and the present practice of art, that what is produced by the seven year old student so conjoined to such factors is a distinctive account of beauty in a consensual, social way. It would also depend on whether we can recognise common identified interests and properties that resonate with aesthetic invocation in the seven year old's painting. Having seen the painting, we are receptive perhaps to the student's particular painterly treatment and configuration of their subject matter. Additionally, what the teacher thought about the student's art work would also depend on whether society thinks this painting exercise can affect the moral well being of its citizens in the world. Estimating what any painting exercise value is, involves noting the intentions and outcomes that are capable of being realised. Society, then, has a stake in the value of the art exercise. Any particular art exercise is seen as valuable when we can derive from it, relevant experiences and external perceptions relating to the intentions and outcomes of the exercise, that further involves concepts, ideas, feelings, actions and imagination that influenced the construction of the art. Furthermore, in any particular art exercise, the social value of it, is to some extent illuminated by the adopted universal norms for forming estimates continuous with particular art practices and individual student interests, capturing in many different ways or not as the case may be, ideal and normal notions of art and life.

Is this art exercise an appropriate way for children to convey their understanding of art, their mental growth, their culture and their goodness? In creating such a painting of their mum and dad, arguably, the child wants to show his or her love for their parents and is this love so expressed valued by the parents, the art world and society? Will the art problems they face be, as Ernst Gombrich asserted, cultural experiments in illusion and from indefinite to more definite perception in later art works (Gombrich, 1960)? An art teacher has to interconnect with the student's way of seeing, hearing, performing and experiencing life in conceptual, spatial, perceptual, physical and cognitive ways related to their capabilities. In that case, a seven year old and the problems that they may be facing when painting a picture of their mum and dad is an entirely different proposition from a mature adult with experience in art. This is a painting exercise in memory and they, like other students in the class, may have no preconceived notion of what they want to represent and how to configure their idea-image in a two dimensional manner, to provide a portrayal of their parents. We can already imagine that this is going to be a challenging exercise in lots of different, important, educational ways.

The art teacher may limit the choice of colours that the student can use for reasons that may relate to prior experiences. Our art teacher may have noticed that more line control and feature control is required to further develop the student's capabilities in their painting exercise. The art teacher might ask their students to identify whether their mum or their dad has black hair, whether they want their parents to be sitting down, standing up, in the garden, in their family car, in bed, mum in the kitchen and dad in the garage (or vice versa) in their paintings. An art teacher might further ask what their mum and dad likes to wear: a dress, shorts, jewellery, tie, and hat. Is the painting going to be mum and dad out with their dog in the park? Are the students themselves going to be in the painting and where will they be placed in their composition? There is an ordered thought process for the painting that the teacher of art is stimulating in timely ways. Furthermore, apart from the important notion that the painting has an 'intention' and that this intention affects the painting creation, the painting still remains a very difficult task of how to project the image that the student has in mind in a perceptual-conceptual feature related physical manner. "At seven years of age, there is accurate right and left judgement and a judgement of visual space, with the self as a reference point.a child learns space concepts by personal involvement, by actually climbing over, hiding behind, running beside, or sitting on top of" (Lowenfeld & Brittain, 1987, p. 229–230). So what we can expect from the student is their ability to draw from this prior experience that in turn will affect aspects of their painting of their mum and dad, assuming that they have this prior experience. As Lowenfeld and Brittain further mention, an art exercise at this age "is a means by which to develop relationships and to make concrete some vague but important thoughts…we are not discussing thinking here as the quiet contemplation of a problem; rather, we are considering total intellectual development, which at this age is nicely infused with fantasy, reality and biological responses to the environment" (Lowenfeld & Brittain, 1987, p. 234). Therefore, the beauty that their painting will have, will be further in proportion to their fantasy, reality, conception and physiological thinking-responses.

This exercise is likely to stir a lot of emotional excitement from the seven year old student, which in a bodily responding manner to the art task can be part of the effective conveying beauty of the painting. Physiological responses as well as cognitive and emotional arousal conjoined to the imagination of the student who holding their paint brush liberally constructs a round head and reacts to the image by wondering how to shape a human body picks up the paint brush once again. However fragmentary, limpid, faulty and broken in an adult art quality way (Lowenfeld & Brittain, 1987, p. 250) the body form represented in such children's art can still be beautiful. We may lack, as adults, not only a generosity of spirit for such art but to narrow a perspective of the eccentricities and the illuminating understanding of the student's delight that invigorates the painting response introducing a benefit to them and a benefit to us having seen the finished student painting. Of how in such an art exercise important images, feelings and needs are being expressed by students who are attempting to seriously convey their love and attain satisfaction from the exercise of things that should not be neglected in a social world, our child like ways of thinking, imagining and perceiving and loving. The teacher of art who has set their students this task knows that their students are familiar with the subject of study (their parents) and are immediately conscious of it. Our art teacher knows that in addition there is a different kind of closeness with the subject matter that has come about only through the external working process in representational form of their mum and dad. There is a level of seeing and experience in relation to what is constructed in the concrete (the shape of things, the colour of things and actual external phenomena selected, for example) that affects perceptions, emotions and cognitions that they are alive to in the creative process which furthers the student`s relation to intelligence, striving to produce more activity, development and delight from the painting exercise. For the parents, their son`s or daughter's painting is a reminder of their preciousness in life, their being in the world and the shared role that they play in the child's life.

As I have mentioned, Dante's *Divine Comedy* is a masterpiece of art but clearly in an art class a seven year old's painting of his mum and dad is never going to be a masterpiece of art. However, we can experience beauty in a seven year old's painting which the teacher has just put up on their classroom wall as high art for the reasons I have stated. Beauty, argued Aristotle, was synonymous with refinement and that meant understanding corresponding to gathering the meaning of things with moral sense. We learn to recognise that there is excellence in a seven year old's art work exercise that is part of a constantly rising standard of development in art education of a continuing normative and ordinary standard of art in the world of a human life, doing what adults also do, learning to enjoy, create, perceive and comprehend works of art. We would be in error, however, if we did not understand that a child's art work is in proportion to their capabilities on the one hand and on the other hand, being able to appreciate this. It is impossible not to admit that this will involve an adult's generosity of spirit being taken by the child's art work, a sense of indebtedness to the art of the child, that pours from their movements, stories and paintings, for example, in ways that reaffirm and heighten the adult's cherished connection to the child's art. Knowing that in a teaching manner, the child's art work is not only a door to more assured adult considerations, but equally for the child, the art work is of great help to them to be able to express their emotional freedom, imaginative feelings and fine motor skills, that, in turn, sheds light on their cheerfulness, preciousness, human sympathy and empowering capabilities.

Consequently, art teaching exercises can preserve the memories, feelings and thoughts of the student that relate to their own experiences of life which on viewing their art work in its representative basic form becomes assessable through the features of it. The student produces a physical impression with character properties in the broadest sense as particular to their mum and dad. They express their self-directed pleasure in creating their images so construed, due, in part, to their discovery of what situations, objects, colours, patterns, shapes, spaces and compositions seem to assert when developing and pondering such issues. To actually determine the value of the student's art, Aristotle asked in his *Poetics*: does the art appeal to the human feeling in us, does it express the right emotions in us and does it move us in common ways and is it significant of being in the world (Halliwell, 1998)? This seems to be a good way to judge art in education and its effectiveness in a welfare maximisation overall manner.

Within many different cultures, seven year old's paintings are highly valued because such work is seen as sometimes "relevant to norms that operate locally" (Eaton, 1995, p. 95–106). Even though we will not find children's art work in the permanently displayed art collections of the *Louvre* in Paris or in the *Museum of Modern Art* in New York, within such art buildings young children are painting and drawing and being encouraged by society to do so. So when we see a fifteen years old's painting of their parents, their critical viewpoint may have been influenced by a Rembrandt self-portrait in ways inconceivable when they were five years old but their five year old's experience of art is no less an achievement than the art they are achieving at fifteen years of age. When a parent puts their seven year old son's or daughter's painting on their refrigerator at home, education is serving their communities in social, scholarly ways. Social existence is strengthened not weakened by this art task, preserving and making in combination what corresponds *a fortiori* to a more beautiful life. We examine individual works of art to decide whether there is beauty in an art production, and whether the idea, music, movement and the thoughts so expressed in art performances have value against a range of criteria suitable for the particular, individual, singular work of art. In much of art practice, as the student develops, particularly at high school: "the art of literature, vocal or written, is to adjust the language so that it embodies what it indicates" (Whitehead in W.H. Auden, 1979, p. 240).

'High culture' divided from 'low culture' is perhaps too demeaning of people's lives and if it exists in order to imply a class artistic-cultural bias we ought to reject it in education on moral, social, intellectual and aesthetic grounds. "Whether anyone prefers D.H. Lawrence to P. G. Wodehouse or thinks more highly of Michael Tippett than Scott Joplin is not to the point. What we want to know is whether the different status frequently accorded to different artistic production has a rational basis or is the result of mere social prejudice and cultural illusion" (Graham, 1995, p. 36).

Shakespeare was no aristocratic writer and nor was Mark Twain. These terms 'high art' and 'low art' represent a taste divide, when what the world needs is more sharing, more sympathetic human feelings, more coming together, more commonality and more community.

When classical writers talk about 'high art' they will sometimes compare one piece of 'high art' with another piece of 'high art' in an attempt to grade what they perceive is the better art work. For example, Homer exceeds Shakespeare in truth; Dante exceeds Shakespeare in loveliness. Mill falls into the same trap when he remarks: "who would not prefer one Virgin and Child of Raphael to all the pictures which Rubens, with his fat, floozy Dutch Venuses, ever painted?" (Mill, 1897, p. 214). There is no rational basis that can substantiate how Homer exceeds Shakespeare in truth just as there is no rational basis that can substantiate how Dante exceeds Shakespeare in loveliness, for it is not like adding numbers together to decide who has got it right and who has got it wrong. As much as I enjoy reading Homer, Dante and Shakespeare and admire Raphael and Rubens, such high art must not be allowed to crowd out a student's experience rendered conscious by reading stories like *Cinderella*. In reading *Cinderella* or Sue Townsend's *The Secret Diary of Adrian Mole Aged Thirteen and Three Quarters* it is not unusual, as David Constantine remarks about Fleur Adcock's poem *For Heidi with Blue Hair,* that in critical ways there can be: "a shock, a quickening of consciousness, a becoming alert to better possibilities, an extension, a liberation, for such poetry is, 'to put it mildly, a useful thing if, when reading it, we sense a better way of being in the world'" (Astley, 2002, p. 22).

"Never did a fancy so teem with sensuous imagery as Shelley's. Wordsworth economises an image, and detains it until he has distilled all the poetry out of it, and it will not yield a drop more: Shelley lavishes his with a profusion which is unconscious because it is inexhaustible. The one like a thrifty housewife, uses all his materials and wastes none, the other scatters them with a reckless prodigality of wealth of which there is perhaps no similar instance" (Mill, 1897, p. 230). Here is a comparison by Mill but no temptation this time to claim Shelley or Wordsworth as the better poet. But this is something that can be troubling for an art teacher too when there is clearly going to be a variety of art work produced by the students in an art class and all of it may be meet the requirements of the art exercise. When several of the drawings are placed opposite each other on an art class wall, each equally can be communicating in relative ways their property perceiving differences. Each drawing can meet the exercise quality requirement standards. The art teacher's task is now how to convince the whole class that different repetitions, tones, lines, shapes, spaces, depths, lighting conditions, depictions, gestures, compositions, abstractions, mark-making techniques and ideas can be given the same grade mark. It has to be shown what is being communicated in the particular, singular, individual art works, together with what they have in common with the other different, particular, singular, individual student art works, involving what can seen, imagined, reasoned and experienced. Understanding how each of the student art works has been composed, the ideas of it and the features and properties each art has expressed and what was placed in the object where and how was it configured, what it represents, and how was the image or concept constructed on the paper: sharply, delicately, burlesquely and in perspective or two-dimensionally? All this can be a difficult task for students to be able to notice these differences, understand different concepts and qualities, discern these and compose solutions appropriate for the art representing equivalent evidences that meet the art requirements.

A student's own conception of their art work or performance may have difficulty seeing, hearing and perceiving outside their own constructed performance and perceptions, similarities with differences in appearances or opposites of equal value in relation to other student art works. Certain aspects may elude them because of their lack of prior experience involving correlative pleasures, cognitions, visions, images and performances. With limited familiarization of different art practices, these nevertheless establish concerns that lie between the next progressive chain of imaginative reasoning and feeling capabilities to better realise and appreciate further qualities of an art.

I feel it is worth briefly returning to Wittgenstein for a few of the reasons why students may have difficulties in noticing differences and similarities in art exercises.

a. "'Is the most important impression which a picture produces a visual impression or not?' 'No. Because you can do things that visually change the picture and yet not change the impression.' This sounds as though one wished to say it wasn't an impression of the eyes: an effect, but not a purely visual effect".

b. "'But it is a visual impression.' Only these are the features of the visual impression which matter, and not the others. Suppose [someone says]: 'Associations are what matter — change it slightly and it no longer has the same associations.' But can you separate the associations from the picture, and have the same thing? You can't say: 'That's just as good as the other: it gives me the same associations'".

c. "Two schools" (1) 'What matters is the patches of colour [and line]'. (2) 'What matters is the expression on these faces'.

d. Wittgenstein goes on to say about the above schools (representing formalism and expressionism): "In a sense, these two don't contradict one another. Only (1) doesn't make clear that the different patches have different importance, and that different alterations have totally different effects: some make all the difference in the world" (Wittgenstein, 1966, p. 34–5).

e. "As far as one can see the puzzlement I am talking about can be cured only by peculiar kinds of comparisons, e.g. by an arrangement of certain musical figures, comparing their effects on us. 'If we put in this chord it does not have that effect; if we put in this chord it does'" (Wittgenstein, 1966, p. 20).

Unobservable differences and paltry conceptual characterizations of an art work can limit what a student can see, think or hear. Equally, a student has invested a lot of time and effort into their art, with a lot of emotional involvement and so naturally

87

an inexperienced student may find it difficult to appreciate how another student in the same class has got the same grade for their art as they have been given. While the theme, the idea or any particular property of an art exercise certainly may be recognisable throughout the whole student class, these factors, we know, will vary from one student to another in relation to the performance, pictorial and poetic expression that each individual has developed. When we introduce and encourage more conceptual and aesthetic freedom in an art task we get more conceptual and aesthetic variety from the students back. The more we discuss art with students, the more likely it is that students will appreciate better, greater and more differences and similarities in art productions. However, this approach is not an adequate teaching approach for the activity of art and a discussion of art. If, for example, the students have spatial problems conceiving and constructing three-dimensional forms in a drawing, like drawing a cube, for example, which is a difficult object to draw; being unable to draw such an object can definitely impact on a whole range of art student related issues. Similar examples can be found in music, drama, dance, literature, poetry, architecture and design practice, where the accomplishment of such a task physically, can open up new concepts, perceptions, imaginative possibilities, hearing, seeing, producing, performing and new thinking. "When I was a student, copying existing works of art was a major part of the curriculum. It was a good thing, you can't do without it. It's learning to draw at the same time; you find out whether you've got an eye that can judge proportions and distances and so on, strengths of black and light, and tone values" (Moore, 1986, p. 40).

High art is not a good enough position, connection and introduction for the teaching of art education. It either takes for granted the importance of our social world or it ignores it. Like a lot of 'high' level theory, sometimes the more important, precious and intelligent things are the simple things habitually exhibited in life. I have indicated that art education is 'high art' because it is steeped in 'high art' conjoined to what students are capable of experiencing and accomplishing and that art in general has a pedigree of thinking about art that reaches back to the Greeks and beyond. I have also indicated that art education is correspondingly 'high art' because what students produce in art education, we recognise in important social ways as 'high art'. I have also indicated that 'high art' is high on the list of teaching and curriculum concerns. That welfare maximisation overall requires 'high art' teaching experience. Yet the student acts of art are the experiences that preserve, develop and project high art. The student's intuitions, passions and resolve affect their regard, playing and creation of an art. Their aesthetic experiences are full of imagination, cognition and understanding with soft, melancholic, joyful, inquisitive, dispassionate and mute reflections of life. The musical production of *Oliver Twist* by Lionel Bart and *The Sound of Music* by Richard Roberts and Oscar Hammerstein are both accompanied by theatrical and choreographed performances and are staged and set directed. In these performances are key continuous evolving concepts of art and life and good and evil representing in ordinary ways "positive acts for the benefit of others" (Mill, 1985, p. 70).

Art education makes it possible for students to gain more confidence and understanding in learner-like ways of the character of things that students bring to view, which Heidegger infers involves understanding more openly and intelligibly objects, relationships and human beings. Of a pair of shoes that Van Gogh painted (of which there were several), Heidegger mentions "in the stiffly rugged heaviness of the shoes there is the accumulated tenacity of her slow trudge through the far-spreading and ever-uniform furrows of the field swept by the raw wind" (Heidegger, 1993, p. 159). Here is an example of that positive act for the benefit of others.

Art education should not limit itself to any form of art and determining notion of art. The triumphs of art viewed in terms of high art consist too of ordinary experiences of art. Ordinary experiences that affect creations of art are so vital, so important, so inspiring and so intelligible for common insight, continuity and stability reasons in life that in a dual manner these imaginative contemplations and aesthetic ideas are good for art education development and are good for society. For Dewey, the relevance of art education and a strong reason why we teach art should be how art reflects daily life, the *genius loci* or the natural expression of a place that is not remote from the "scope of the common or community life" (Dewey, 1980, p. 6). His point is that art education should stand in connection with the integrated meanings and mechanisms of social life, revealing in different ways what awakens our human association through the display of the student's art. The student, through their character of thought and actions, makes the art object speak and in doing so, the student has determined and expressed an aesthetic view.

High art is what art must be in education. Louis Arnaud Reid states: "the aesthetic outlook draws upon the inescapably metaphorical character of ordinary sense perception—ordinary, that is, when we are not looking at things for some special purpose, as in some scientific observations where we are concerned with bare value-free facts only, abstracted from feelings and emotions [perhaps imagination too] about them. We look at the clouds: they are 'lowering', 'threatening' or the landscape is 'serene', the sunshine 'cheerful'. Jagged outlines are 'harsh', colours 'gay' or 'sombre', the flotsam on the tide floats 'wearily' leaves 'tremble'. The Grand Canyon is charged with significance of vast emotional depth. The creative visual artist shares in this infinite plenitude of daily sensuous-symbolic significance—perhaps more intensely because it is a central preoccupation of his daily life. Added to it is the other unlimited plenitude of the potential symbolism of his media" (Reid, 1986, p. 18).

Some common understandings of life with moral estates of it, as Kant indicates, may involve "buildings and trees majestic or stately, or plains laughing and gay; even colours are called innocent, modest, soft, because they excite sensations containing something analogous to the consciousness of a state of mind produced by moral judgements" (Kant, 1928, §. 59). A social moral view of art education does not correspond to a conservative, traditional, aristocratic or even an avant-garde practice of art but rather as a curriculum of art divided between autonomy, integration, adjustment, accommodation, consensual, cooperative and opposition thoughts receptive to human association and shared experiences of the commonplace.

Dance, as an element of drama, rhythm, imitation, expression, conceptualisation and choreographic choices, can be seen as part of one's mutual, communicative feelings, desires, affections, and perceptions forming part of a group identity of interests in life that by analogue represent some fellowship of values to indicate grief, fear, gracefulness, romanticism, coldness, a grave image, contemptable behaviour, gratitude, a fantastical, dreamy presentation or a moving force of body movement actions that appear to be thrusting aside imagined barriers. Dance, as Noël Carroll notes, "has perenially functioned as a means to commemorate events, such as rites of passage, weddings, presidential inaugurations, alliances, bar mitzvahs, and preparations for war; to propitate gods and other forces of nature, as in rain dances and fertility celebrations; and to recall historical occurences, including victories, revelations, the changing of the seasons.In many societies, dance also figured in informal contexts as a means to entertainment, pleasure, and self-expression, though even in thes cases, the dance often—albeit not always-subservices a large social function such as courtship or socialability (e,g, square dancing). Indeed, it has been suggested that dance serves a very deep purpose in tradtional societies, coordinating the activities beween them. Thus, dance can be an instrument, whether sacred or profane, in the instilling and reinforcing of social bonds within a culture" (Carroll, 2005, p. 583).

There are just far too many artists in the world of 'high art' past and present that extol the virtues of their childhood associated aesthetic art experiences. Whether in music, literature, dance or design, for example, there are many artists in these fields who recall features, incidents, passions and events of their childhood experiences that play upon the sensibilities of some of their mature art works. Tentative points of physiological reception may present itself in a tune, dance movement, image and thought, forming an immediate association of an incident in childhood that combined to vibrate the delight in hearing 'this', for example, to confidently become a little bit of the character of the art. Years of reading children stories in bed and giggling to oneself in the process can be the experience that still affects the ideas of the mature artist's work. Childhood experiences not only open the doors for more sophisticated art production but the self-same artist may also attempt to retain that freshness, that intuitiveness, that spontaneity, that memory, that simplicity, that devilishness, that cunningness, that intensity, that strangeness of looking and feeling, that playfulness, that capacity to love everything, that stupidity, that carefree attitude, that deficiency, that moodiness, that giggling, that awakening, that wonder and that innocence.

I have deliberately avoided painting a picture of art in education that expresses any suggestion that the higher qualities of art in education are synonymous with elitist, avant-garde or bourgeois ideas of art. Rather, I feel I have painted a picture where the qualities of art are social, moral, intellectual, practical and aesthetic. Within movements of art, however, are the expressed qualities of different art notions. High art is not purely Renaissance art any more than low art is Pop art, because high art is endemic of art generally, not just Renaissance art and 'low art' is a pejorative term disingenuous to Pop art, which is also a high art. If the art is sophisticated, it will have the kind of qualities we admire about the art.

Students' sophisticated understanding of art in capability ways exhumes the important qualities and experiences of art and life which, while ordinary and elementary, are substantive. For another example of this: "the first poems I knew were nursery rhymes, and before I could read them for myself I had come to love just the words of them, the words alone. What the words stood for, symbolized, or meant, was of very secondary importance; what mattered was the sound of them as I heard them for the first time on the lips of the remote and incomprehensible grownups who seemed, for some reason, to be living in my world. And these words were, to me, as the notes of bells, the sounds of musical instruments, the noises of wind, sea, and rain, the rattle of milk carts, the clopping of hooves on cobbles, the fingering of branches on a windowpane, might be to someone, deaf from birth, who has miraculously found his hearing. I did not care what the words said, overmuch, nor what happened to Jack and Jill and the Mother Goose rest of them; I cared for the shapes of sound that their names, and the words describing their actions, made in my ears; I cared for the colours the words cast on my eyes." (Thomas, 1979, p. 184). It is this, and not notions of high art or low art, that is more representative of the norms of art in educational practice having strong connections to welfare maximisation overall for society. It is this sort of continuity, as an example, that is vital because it affects all art and students' development in art education. Conjointly, art activity expresses familiarity, commonality, togetherness and shared experiences; it cements the importance of art in life as Dylan Thomas implies; art experience expresses the values that we cherish, hug, cry, laugh and love in existence. There is nothing unsophisticated and frivolous about any of this confirming life that Thomas recollects. Our world crumbles in all kinds of dysfunctional ways when such sophistication is unappreciated by society.

True enough, some Hollywood movies are 'low art' but not all Hollywood movies are 'low art', lots of TV programmes are 'low art', but a few of them occasionally are not. What Thomas describes as his childhood experience of art is not only an important common experience but moreover it draws attention approximately to the 'laws' of what constitutes 'high art' experience because Thomas quite clearly is establishing the fact that these experiences are the comedies, tragedies, romances, landscapes, conversations, abstractions, seascapes, objects, rhythms and poetry of art that reflect life. The enjoyable aspects of our lives can be broad enough reflecting our simple pleasures and our higher pleasures presented in delightful-meaningful ways in art educational exercises. Fine works of art can be produced from the most simple and mundane and ordinary experiences of life. We know this from art history: Katsushika Hokusai's colour woodblock: *South Wind, Clear Sky* (1830–33); Willy Ronis's photograph *Little Parisian* (1952); Pieter Brueghel's *Wedding Breakfast* (1557); Vincent van Gogh's *Cypresses* (1889) and much of Paul Cézanne's art work, for example. But no one in their right minds would call any of these artists ordinary or simple. The terms 'high' culture and 'low' culture is not something that is recognised as a social distinction by the North American aboriginal communities and their artists, who believe that all art defines them culturally, whether the aboriginal artist is a painter, sculptor, jeweller, ceramist, textile designer, boat builder, box maker, tool maker or a house builder, for example.

A child's nature simultaneously possesses a social nature and the earliest representative signs that art is social are the Palaeolithic paintings in the Lascaux Caves in France. To describe art as either 'high art' or 'low art', or 'high art' versus 'popular art' are unsuitable terms for what occurs in the production of art in education, where the production of art in education is concerned with the quality of art that the student produces drawing upon social, moral, intellectual, practical and aesthetic concerns.

A student's sophisticated experience starts very early in life, when, for example, young children are taken to a concert performance of Beethoven's *Symphony No. 9*. They may understand it perfectly. How can a young child understand perfectly a work of such 'high art'? Put aside the fact that they are not musically trained, though they may have already begun the process of learning to play a musical instrument and read music, put aside the fact that they may not speak German, put aside the fact that they are inexperienced in life, put aside the fact that they are intellectually very young and put aside the fact that they do not know anything about Beethoven or his music. On the face of it they are hardly sophisticated human beings. But we would be wrong to suggest, for reasons previously discussed, that although they lack important critical factors in refinement, their responses to Beethoven's *Symphony No. 9* are often what we would expect from them and are not too different from adult experiences. A moment ago I said that children can understand Beethoven's *Symphony No. 9* 'perfectly'. This is because they can show all the signs that display a significant, intense, dynamic, in-tune, cognitive-body, aesthetic experience to the music. They may dance to the music, use their hands gesturally, get very excited, emotionally involved, they may listen intensely and be overcome by sense of awe. They smile and giggle, unmasked feelings are expressed, they hum the music's tunefulness, become galvanised by it, offer without too much thought a creative suggestion about the music, present something we had not imagined, reveal different perspectives of the music and show considerable signs that they have paid attention to the music.

When given the opportunity within aesthetic education to experience such art insights (and all students really need to have more of them), to enjoy an art of central importance that puts them at ease with the world of what subsequently stimulates their feelings, imagination and thoughts in a situational context revealing and acquainting them with the kind of experiences that bring people together, these occasions can naturally transform student discoveries about art, reciprocally involving impulses of self and impulses from the world of music as quite normal reactions of life. Their awareness and physical movement in listening to the music can be decisive in shaping the student consciousness of their lives in possible superabundant ways. In one sense a child's aesthetic experiences are indispensible in realising who they are, for the thoughts, feelings and movement they express are extensions of themselves. Their public display in these matters is of substantial educational importance: their listening, their seeing, their love, that smile, that awe, that excitement, that gesture, that dance, that sense of its tune-rhythm and that unmasked or unfelt feeling, that re-acted feeling and thought, of what a cultural, expressive and social life should be.

Adults can have problems with aesthetic responses too, due I think to too much practical thinking, too much economic emphasis, vacant lives, dim retreats and stifled happiness. Cognition suffers. An adult is more likely to be aware that they live in an ugly environment. There is no neighbourhood 'here', because they live in a brutish, turbulent world, because there is little sharing of ennobled genuine affections, because they may be caught up in a rat-race of meaningless human experiences that then distort their ability to change things about themselves. Adults, quite often, can deny themselves such experiences and in denying themselves such experience their cognitive-emotional and ethical existence takes a hit. We walk home from a musical concert of Beethoven's *Symphony No. 9* feeling inspired and rejuvenated. These experiences like awe, solace and love are sophisticated human responses. Music, like all art subjects is a felt-thought physical experience but when children and adults listen to Beethoven's *Symphony No. 9*, go to the theatre to watch Shakespeare's *A Midsummer-Night's Dream*, take part in a dance class or a painting class, for example, the children and the adults will go home feeling like human beings. In such felt-thought aesthetic experiences, we feel ourselves more reinvigorated and real.

The poet, playwright and philosopher Friedrich Schiller who wrote the poem *Ode to Joy* that Beethoven set to music in 1824, argued in his *Aesthetic Letters* for the restoration and harmony of our aesthetic cultivation for a better citizenry notion of well-being in life. We forget how refined children can be and how correspondingly, an aesthetic experience can make a huge difference in people's lives. In education the problem we have is how to keep art activities in the curriculum, develop them and make them more relevant with diminishing resources and diminishing understanding of the importance of art for personal and communal life.

We experience Beethoven's *Symphony No. 9* in ways we take for granted, or most of us do some of the time. It isn't just that this marvelous symphony gives me goose bumps every time I listen to it, it isn't just that this is 'high culture', it is more the fact that young and old alike however 'inexperienced' or experienced their aesthetic pleasures are, all interact with the music in widely and deeply shared ways. Being unwilling and unaware of distinctions between a child's response and an adult's own response, enables us to come together harmoniously absorbed by the musical experience adequate of our cognition, feelings and imagination. This is not utility, this is not music theory, this is not about how rationally intelligent we are, this is not about how clever we are or how politically astute we are, but instead, it is an interlocked irrefutable experience about how life in a certain way can be and ought to be on occasion; a wholeness of inner and outer self-awareness. This isn't science, this isn't mathematics, this is art aesthetic experience. Far too often, instead of restoring commonality, disputes break out between culture and society, which as Friedrich Schiller implies in his *Aesthetic Letters*, come between feelings, cognition and morality, without stopping to think that feelings, cognition and morality can in unison, overlap and combine reciprocally in fruitful submerged and conferred upon action ways, "of a compact dictated by humanity itself" (Kant, 1928, §. 49).

We do not always need to judge, as teachers, a student's art work, to formulate our responses in ways that show how smart we are, when a gentle conversation and a little more human sympathy might be more appropriate. Aesthetically, there are moments in a classroom when the right response may only need in a more complete human way to look at one another in order to know that substantially we have lots in common. We show the student what to do with a camera because this is one way we communicate in art teaching. For a group of 16–18 year old students who already possess some basic photographic skills, the art teacher notices that it is time for them to develop further their skills or risk what they have already gained, while also noticing their enthusiasm for more photography teaching input. They decide ambitiously that it would be good idea if the students could capture photographically the environment in which they live and the landscape of it adequate to the idea that their photographs reflect 'a sense of place'. The art teacher might show them, for example, Fay Godwin's photographs that accompanied Ted Hughes poems of *Elmet* (Hughes & Godwin, 1979). They discuss Godwin's choice of view points, picture shapes and picture emphasis, focal lengths and depth of fields, lighting qualities, textures, tonal control, subject matter, pictorial thinking and the particular scenes she has chosen in relation to Ted Hughes' poems. It is put to the student group, whether they think that Godwin has imaginatively identified with a sense of place meaningfully in an intelligent empathetic manner. Would the undertaking of this project alter student consciousness, move them in a particular way, restore and refine their artistic sentiments and change their views of their environment because they were being asked to observe, create through engagement, reflect, show emergence and their spur of action, experience and self-realise with their own voices and identifications, while responding to conditions, occurrences and situations to thus convey what their sense of place possesses and communicates?

So does it matter that the students share their art aesthetic ideas, their thinking and their way of expressing that is their own? Does it matter that we, like them, take enormous pleasure from many works of art? In the sharing of an aesthetic pleasure by playing, for example, the cello piece that the teacher wants the student to play 'in this way', the teacher of art realises in such moments how sensitive and delicate human beings are, how a different subtle sound of music to the ear can make all the difference. Music does this as all art activity does this; it expresses the intricate, through higher faculties in proportion to student capabilities. In this musical moment, all tension can be released, all difficulty forgotten, the students forget themselves, thoughts blend, spontaneity occurs, without effort, intricate feelings and interactions occur, invention occurs, without force they can feel more restored, more like human beings. The student picks up their bow and with more confidence than before, plays their cello piece like the teacher asked for.

In the flow and in realisation of what is stirring the heart, when sitting there or standing there listening in the park, concert hall or on the high street to a performance of Beethoven's *Symphony No. 9* as a contented human being, we feel the reward of the art. The child's experience and the adult's experience as a strong affective response evoked by the music; cognition and emotion become integrated. Life appears spontaneously as a true conception of a community. Aristotle's notion of an art's catharsis erupts, recognition and pathos is experienced and humanity's impulse is alive and commonly confirmed, the child and the adult feel connected and at ease with the world. Thus education cannot regard this experience as anything other than a quality experience of life normal for the child and the adult to possess. If life is going to mean anything to them, their cognition contributes to an "alignment of the emotions with the perception of moral qualities in the world" (Halliwell, 1998, p. 196), important for human development.

When art movements create new conceptual directions in art, these conceptions are based on ideas about art and life and if we were to investigate the history of art the changes that have occurred in art are influenced by many diverse ideas which puts another hole in the idea of 'high art' and 'low art'. There is consistency and unpredictability of the effects of life upon the ideas of art through the self-made and self-observed incidents, feelings, character and events deliberately seen and thought of. Transforming the feeble, vibrant, pathetic, nebulous, ignorant, humorous, resistant, beautiful and ugly, whose appearance in art which may be simple but the idea very original or whose appearance in art is immensely rich visually but the idea very conventional. One can do good things in art, argued Cézanne, by not doing very much. Cézanne felt that what a young artist must strive to achieve is a good method of construction trained through their own feelings and thoughts in front of nature. So 'high art' or 'low art' has nothing to do with the teaching of art activity, which does not mean, for example, that Cézanne was not influenced by the likes of Michelangelo, Raphael and Tintoretto. He was enormously influenced by these giants in art history, but he maintained that he did not want to be correct in theory but instead correct in front of nature (Kendall, 1988, p. 238). We can describe Cézanne as somewhat representative of a true view of art, which is that one should develop one's own painterly view of art, through one's own experiences and passions of art.

A student who is in a rock band, a jazz band, a quartet or a rap band at school may be doing him or herself a world of good when learning to play an instrument (sensitively and appreciatively), learning to develop their skills (sensitively and appreciatively) and perhaps learning music theory (sensitively and appreciatively).

A novel, a piece of music, a dance or play may be full of high art and low art, features and incidents involving rough, ignorant elements and articulate elements, where the rough, ignorant elements like the articulate elements have been sophisticatedly employed.

Any student of art may find bits of their art production rather straightforward, requiring only minimum attention in their performance. This can be due to their familiarity of the task that has come from plenty of prior readjusting of their cognition, perception and actions from learner-like developmental exercises. Having learnt what a metaphor is and applying it in lots of different sophisticated ways the same task was once very difficult to perform because the student had not yet mastered the art of it. Is learning to play baa-baa-black sheep on a recorder, 'low art'? Is the poem 'Twinkle, twinkle little star.' low art? How about: "The Rum Tum Tugger is a curious cat" (T.S. Eliot); "The Owl and the Pussy-Cat went to sea" (Edward Lear); "Wherever I am, there's always Pooh" (A.A. Milne); "The ants are walking under the ground and the pigeons are flying over the steeple and in beween are the people" (Elizabeth Madox Roberts, *Under the Tree*); "Mother likes the flocks and hats and pretty stuff and coloured mats" (Rose Fyleman, *Gay Go Up*); "I know a little cupboard, with a teeny tiny key, and there's a jar of lollipops, for me, me me" (Walter de la Mare, *The Cupboard*); "By the shores of Gitche Gumee, by the shinning Big-Sea-Water, stood the wigwam of Nokomis. Daughter of the moon, Nokomis" (H.W. Longfellow, *The Song of Hiawatha*). "Some times I help my dad work on our automobile, we unscrew the radiator cap and we let some water run—swish—from a hose in the tank" (Dorothy Baruch, *I Like Machinery*), "A train is a dragon that roars through the dark" (Rowenda Bennett, *Songs from Around a Toadstool Table*); "My mother has the prettiest trick of words and words and words. Her talk comes out as smooth and sleek as breast of singing birds" (Anna Hempstead Branch, *From Shoes that Dance*); "Nothing grows in our garden, only washing" (Dylan Thomas, *Under Milk Wood*): "Twas brillig, and the slithy toves, did gyre and gimble in the wabe" (Lewis Carroll, *Jabberwocky*); "I love chocolate cake. And when I was a boy, I loved it even more" (Michael Rosen, *Chocolate Cake*); "How do I love thee? Let me count the ways" (Elizabeth Barrett Browning, *Sonnets from the Portuguese*): "Double, double toil and trouble; fire burn, and cauldron bubble. Scale of dragon, tooth of wolf, witch's mummy, maw and gulf" (Shakespeare, *Macbeth*); and "All along the backwater, through the rushes tall, ducks are a-dabbling, up tails all!" (Kenneth Grahame, *The Wind in the Willows*). These very short extracts speak volumes about what binds us to common ordinary experiences and acts that are attached to splended feelings, intellectual awareness, imagination and the sensibilities of life that are of social relevance. If we viewed such poetry as 'low art' the nature of poetry itself is called into question, the poetry that can inspire children's being in the world in ways that are good for society.

In art education, any student of art would have learnt that often they cannot achieve what they want to achieve without recourse to their elementary performing productive experiences of an art (this is also the same for a professional artist). They learnt not to take their elementary experiences for granted because under given circumstances this is what may be required to avoid being drawn in too quickly into a task they are not quite ready for without first consolidating a range of primary tasks of an art. Rudimentary aspects of an art in action under given circumstances, mastered at a certain level stimulate the next step when the student is ready to move on. To be able to move on, often requires a chain of previous events, actions and thoughts involving having learnt simple rudimentary actions which correspondingly aid another impression-advance movement capability. Hence simple actions are not only required in order to complete an exercise for this 'dance' movement, for example. In itself the power of it once learnt can imaginatively externalise other uses of it in a variety of extending ways. Paul Klee's teachings at the Bauhaus often explored the power of simple things and their resonances (Klee, 1953). Having learnt how to play the note C on a recorder, this can additionally support further note hearing, more powerful and colourful when played that it may serve other imaginative ideas in the art's musical performance, promoting other features-actions taken in the art to increase note playing understanding. Without having accomplished the playing of the C note the music playing might not have been able to move forward.

For any artist it is not 'high art' or low art' that matters, but crucially the fact they freely draw upon anything to stimulate their art thinking in order to makes ends for themselves in art production. William Blake certainly thought so, but Blake was trained in art, went to art school and was an apprentice print maker. Young students need an awful lot of freedom and the teacher of art has to identify with this experience. Yet structure and content and stimulation may come from 'can you dance like a fish swims through a river', 'can you hear the chuck-chuck sound of a steam engine in this musical beat'? Snakes, cupcakes, shoes, socks, bicycles, birds, rocks, plants, gardens, factories, a clock tower, a door knob, a light bulb, buttons, materials and songs, dances and people in mind past and present from all communities, "a smile, a sudden roguish expression…a glance, a fleeting ray of light" (Hegel, 1988, p. 163), a story that is read around a campfire, a holiday, a playfulness experience of life and an act of inhumanity can all transform an art production; but not of themselves. It takes the student's ability to apprehend themselves in the process of what they are doing, in order to express forms of life and meaning in the world. In art practice, aesthetic experiences, techniques and conceptions need constant attention and adjustment to the world around the student but in the story they tell or the image they produce or the music they perform or the object they make, the presentation of such art production coincides with its free deployment of the students' imagination aligned to their cognition with the power of judgment "consonant with understanding" (Kant, 1928, §. 50) that their capabilities possess.

Quality in art education means that students explore their culture in sensitive, thoughtful and imaginative ways corresponding to the task objectives and outcomes of the art exercise. The student's individual inclinations influence their art's creation-performance. Cultural diversity through art assists the student's understanding of a wide range of different qualities of art. A student paints a bunch of flowers, another student plays the violin in a school orchestra to the theme of Star Wars, another student, while all this is going on, is in the school library reading Roald Dahl's *George's Marvellous Medicine*, and while in the library with the windows open they hear one of their friends rehearse in an adjacent room singing the Beatles song *All You Need is Love,* for the school's forthcoming concert. Tomorrow, another student will find out that the school has selected them to play the role of the Artful Dodger in the musical version of Charles Dickens' *Oliver Twist.* He will be accompanied by many of his school friends in supporting roles as part of Fagin's pickpocketing gang. Other students may go on later in life to design furniture, clothes, jewellery, cars, lighting, buildings and fabrics, for example. Would we regard any of this necessarily as 'low art'? Whether its Mark Twain, Emily Brontë, Doris Lessing, Alice Walker, John Steinbeck, Jack London, Herman Melville, Jacoba van Heemskerck or Jacqueline du Pré on the cello or a fabric design by William Morris, the delights of the high and the low qualities of life are explored in appreciative ways. William Morris wrote an essay expressing a view for a wider interpretation of high art in his 1878 paper, *The Lesser Arts* (Morris, 1979, p. 31–56).

The refinement of art may come from the subject-matter of the art exercise itself but in the teaching of art the student has to understand it, be stimulated by it and be thrilled, questioning and appreciative. If the art production is crude or trivial this may not be because the subject-matter was of 'low art'. The subject-matter might be of 'high art', because tragedy was the theme, but in performance the tragedy was crudely presented. What makes good art is the conception, often the result of understanding accompanied by imaginative insight and empathy. There is no such thing as 'low art' though we might describe a particular piece of student art work as poorly conceived. But if we did, the criticism would be grounded in aesthetic criticism or moral criticism of it or both. If the criticism was aesthetic criticism and or moral criticism, and the student then acted on the aesthetic-moral criticism adjusting their ideas, performance, written work, or sculptural piece accordingly, there is a very good chance when seeing these changes made to the art production, that we can now discern a more sophisticed body of work in relative capability ways.

Art education focuses on the quality of the student's art work, the teaching qualities of an art, students' interests and their capabilities and conjointly the demands of a curriculum of art. However to repeat, the quality of art produced by students, will be judged in aesthetic, intellectual, moral, practical and social ways by the art teacher. Aesthetic life is common in the world and art activity formally reflects this and in ascending learner-like ways supports students' human life in dignified pleasurable productions "beyond that of tickling the ear" (Mill, 1897, p. 201).

To recap, while personally I do not like the terms 'high-art' and 'low art', I would want to say assuredly that a student never produces 'low art', or if they do this is very rare in an art educational lesson. This is because an art lesson is all about 'high art' everything in the lesson is all about 'high art' experience and activity. A teacher of art never teaches 'low art' because the curriculum of art is a social construction of 'high art' conceptions of the practices of art. Of course, a teacher of art may find some faults with the student's art but not necessarily do anything about these faults in their artwork. An adult's point of view of the student's art may quite correctly be inappropriate in a learner-like way as Lowenfeld and Brittain remark. Through a series of further exercises the student's incorrectness may naturally disappear. Finding faults with students' art is inevitable and is a regular occurrence, but in asking a student to 'play again for me this piece of music but this time gently touch the notes on the piano' is 'high art' thinking and the student of art in an art lesson always makes a genuine attempt at producing 'high art'.

There is no contradiction when the art teacher points out to a student that their art work-performance is very good, while keeping to themselves that the student still has much to improve upon and develop over time. They are focused on producing 'high art' and the art teacher who engages regularly with their students in art discussions, directs, shows, demonstrates, encourages and facilitates 'high art' thinking and performance. Whether it is a group of women making a quilt for their hospital, whether it is a child reading Goscinny and Sempé's *Nicholas on Holiday* or whether it is a drawing and painting class at school centred around items of personal significance to the student, all this is 'high art' involvement. Whether it is degree product design students building robots in their university studio, degree craft students producing glass blowing kitchenware objects or theatre students at university putting on a performance of *Grease* the musical, whether is it a ceramic cup exercise in a pottery school class, whether it is producing a dress in the school's fashion and textile room, whether it is group of students learning to play the drums, violin, saxophone, tin whistle or the guitar in a school music class, singing carols as part of the school's choir, a Scottish country dance or the African warrior dance *Agbekor*; none of these experiences and activities are 'low art', but instead can be seen as salient activities of 'high art'.

CONCLUSION

The dryness of the human soul.

(Malraux, 1978, p. 630)

The arts open our eyes and ears to the world. Any nation's prosperity involves how art in education fosters the common good. I have argued that education is failing to realise the importance of art education. Hampered by a lack of confluence and pragmatism to unlock what art in education can achieve is pretty clear evidence that profiting from the instruction of an art carries little educational weight. The recent self-exceptionalist notions of art as guardianships of art have departed from promoting what is of mutual advantage to it: the normal, continuous and regular occurring social benefits of art in education relating to welfare maximization overall issues. Self-exceptionalism in art is sometimes of uncertain status and "may be taken in a good as well as in a bad sense" (Hume, 1965, p. 48) when considering that art is of greater public value when it serves education welfare maximization overall issues. Poor educational policy judgments have lead to the uncultivation of human affairs in education. Art education is not a luxury but a necessity for knowing ourselves better, as the Greek Oracle implies, for fashioning existence superiorially that is of the public good. As Hume mentions it has always been "more easy to account for the rise in the progress of commerce" (Hume, 1965, p. 73) in any society than it has been to recognise in interconnected complementary ways of no less importance, the inculcation of an arts education that is of enormous social benefit to society to brighten up any face of sorrow, happiness, sympathetic feeling and intelligence. There is every reason to believe, as Hume suggests, and as I have been explaining, how art education can "operate like the sun" (Hume, 1965, p. 112). In exemplifiable ways I have discussed some of the learner-like, accountable, teaching instances that can prevail in art education to reassuringly manifest the emulations and accomplishments of art that are of common benefit representing convincing proofs of our close intercourses in the world.

In my introduction I remarked: why should we teach art and how should we teach art? I asserted that while it is very important to have a skills focus and a conceptual focus like 'the virtues of ambiguity in art...' the genus of why we should teach art in education and how we should teach art in education activity rests primarily on its social effectiveness retaining, engaging and beholding the higher qualities of art in education. Art education needs to step-up and embrace more of our common life with insights coming from the art production. For surely what we want to see from the arts in education is the cultivation of social disposition and reasoning enjoying moral, imaginative, intellectual and human sympathetic feelings. What is naturally occurring, conveying information in a free-play manner, stimulating students' thoughts and actions needs refinement by continuous teaching exercises bringing together and combining concepts, ideas and representational treatments that can cause appropriate student development. Yet colours, patterns, textures, rhythms, tones, words and movements may have no resemblance or representational qualities but consist nevertheless of qualities, concepts, ideas, emotions, imaginations and evocations in viable ways due to the way colours, patterns, textures, rhythms, tones, words and movements have constructively been expressed. Imaginative distinctions related to experiences we can perceive moving us in agreeable and insightful ways can help us understand and create the affinities, possibilities, capabilities and temperament of others needed, for example, when we consider deeds and actions portrayed in a play. In art education when students are exploring freely ideas, observations, accents, rhymes, intensities, feelings and original notions of an art, they are doing so in relation to intentions and outcomes. It is specifically ideas and notions capable of bringing home to us our compassions and feelings of relief, excitement and awakening that carry our sentiments and aspirations, limiting and extending the conceptual and outward appearances of an art expressing a worth we can agree on that has purport and significance for human beings extorting approval in learned and pleasurable, overlapping ways. Arts education should be on a par with science education and the fact that they are not weakens all manner of commonality, happiness, esteem and erudition. Without art, life can push us to the edge without never knowing it, is one way to interpret Sophocles' *Antigone*.

I have discussed why I believe the social aspect of art in education is not an irrelevant concept in the idea of art. Nothing could be further from the truth as the vast majority of historical and contemporary art production is designed to appeal to us in this accustomed manner. Art activity has always been interested in articulating, showing and revealing life's social existence in accord with its variable world consciouness, corresponding to life and art of one's time but with the continuity that although the world changes many things remain unchanged too as Søren Kierkegaard explains in *The Tragic in Ancient Drama, Reflected in the Tragic in Modern Drama* (Kierkegaard, 1987). The social productions and performances of art in education are not a side-issue of art but are central and investigative points of references about art and the conscious acts of its capable and variable learner-like considerations. The delights of which universally appeal in common ways affecting our higher understanding of life, so forming the communicated scenes and incidences that explain what we can agree about an art that is good for us generally. What is generally good for us like reading Dostoyevsky's *Crime and Punishment*, for example, is a way "to get back into the world" (Merleau-Ponty, 1964, p. 159). Incidentally, Einstein believed he learnt more from Dostoyevsky's *Crime and Punishment* than from any scientific study he undertook as a student. Art experience sets our mental powers and feelings into swing under teaching guidance that influences affections appropriate to objects and their appearances. From all manner of an arts history past and present, of rank, idea and character in the arts creation, the student through pedagogic input can learn naturally what sinks in, in relation to the art activity that advances with particular, common and general differences affixing thoughts, ideas and feelings that contain relevant conceptions that are also shared and discussed in a class. Exploring the student reflections in a class situation, as Hume mentions, involves the merits and demerits of the art work; the excitement, spontaneity and passion that can have a real effect on the art work; the purpose of the art exercise and the goals of it; the wisdom and folly of how things in appearance were treated, played and organized; the virtues and vices of certain character portrayals that strengthen the art work; the properties and features of the art work that are cognitive and prudent and reciprocally the enjoyment, invention and eloquence of the art production.

An art's social connection is an art's strength, not its weakness. One cannot be teaching art independent of one of the most influential factors upon art creation; common life, as Walt Whitman (1986) argues in *Leaves of Grass*. Ordinary existence, as I have suggested, is such a large part of intellectual, moral, creative and aesthetic consciousness securing contingently when combined the higher pleasures that give stability, continuity and conversely change for understanding social cohesion, independence and personal well-being. It isn't having a taste for art that is quintessentially important but rather that art education enables us to express our feelings, cognitions, perceptions and actions bestowing the postulates that have an attraction corresponding to the fullness and richness of life that affects human happiness letting us and presupposing that we should look beyond merely ourselves to what can act on our mind and emotions advancing social existence. Art education deserves more attention because it can successfully apprehend parts of the mutual relations we have that beget private and public life, of judgments capable of unifying aspects of being in the world, keeping it alive, inducing, possessing and fitting to sound common understandings of being in the world. We might reasonably judge how good art education is by the breadth and depth of teaching in art generating insights generously into existence, facilitating and approving our sympathetic feelings for others and our individuality in the world coming together and cooperating as a determinate of self-related proper existence, a genuine character act of oneself, forming an understanding of a community and seeing the common good as a constituted power of oneself. As we know, students in art education get the opportunity to act-out or to do a painting exercise for example, of a subject that is common to them but to express it seeking to recognise and compare through external modes that are adjusting as more comprehension and activity in appearance is occurring, learning to estimate imaginatively how best to perform, represent and conceptualise what they have been asked to act-out or paint. Drawing flowers, foxes, shapes and twigs, making a dress, reading a Roald Dahl novel, playing a musical instrument and reading music theory and performing on stage a Mark Twain short story are, for example, instances that can enhance our human happiness beyond bare delight, when containing impressions addressed to ourselves but with the training aspects of an art that compels us to explore the finer touches of reasoning, observation, imagination, capriciousness, laughter, opposition and sentiment appropriate to the work.

The variety of ways theatre, music, poetry, literature, design, fashion, dance, crafts, film, photography, sculpture, architecture and painting can penetrate illuminatingly in pleasurable ways our points of union and disunion with the world are no mean feats of excellence. Great artists have always done so and students' art work of a different degree are taught the physical conditions, concepts, reasons, imagination and ideas that deal with different learner-like judgements of art for grasping and comparing individual comprehensions of people, places, events, actions, sounds, movements and objects that is the art's exposition of things. Our wider community benefits from an art's historical viewpoint, developing and evolving evidence of the alternating attractions of art which in appearance is life's kindred social spirit involving past and present, different cultural ideas of art conjoined to the instances of family life, care in the community, love, comfort, work, desires, fantasies, beauty, sexuality, identity, landscapes, city life, a storm at sea, an imaginary figure, a summer's day, inequality, danger, tragedy and murder. Manifest in representations of art activity are the deductive thoughts of the student performing and presenting plausible actions, movements, conceptions, ideas, feelings and images in accord with justifying the features, qualities and properties that supply, by understanding them in analogous ways, what their art competently has accomplished. To recap, it is in the nature of teaching that what students ought to do in order to carry out successfully the learning task is, on the one hand, explained to them by the teacher in ways the students can understand and on the other hand what the art product exhibits, as the students are producing it, is an estimate of their consciousness and conceptual abilities with a willingness to take further action on reflection related to their formed art as it is occurring, adapted to what they have produced with further teaching on-going conversations explaining how to improve their art production. The teacher of art has to sensibly judge all manner of indeterminateness in the student's art production. I have shown that in art education there is a clear process and range of developmental learner-like art activities, and that in these art activities with their corresponding outcomes are the benchmarked norms befitting what student capabilities can achieve. Whatever the performance or object of the lesson is, the student class ought, as a whole, to be able to succeed in what they undertake. Motivation, considerateness, kindness, cognition, imagination, perception, feeling, physical properties and actions, as I have discussed, are key factors in art education activity.

I have also attempted to explain how a teacher of art and a student of art in normal situational ways interact that is of relevance to the higher quality constructing and performing experiences of an art that in associable ways are what we recognise as plausible and precise observations. We can speak accurately about the art treatment and ideas themselves and of the conversations and identifications of one kind and another of life imagined and made real by association which is then capable of exciting in us, shared common agreements. The student is not just getting an education in art, which outrageously is what some people think, but in connection, in a coalescing manner, they are benefitting from the effects of an education fruitful for social accord .

The art teacher knows that art activity needs aesthetic freedom in order for the student to have recourse, as Kant remarks, to any boundless experience of their furtherance of life, to weigh the matter of art for themselves, and to assert outlooks evoked by the art's physical conditions and their cognitions of it that affect the construction and modifications of a script, theme, topic, idea or musical work production, for example. To those aspects of appearances to which the pedagogical ideas are applied involving the shapes, lines, curves, symbols, phrases, scenes, stories, abstractions, concepts, moral notions, colours, styles, tones, movements and musical performances of all manner of associated heightened life which increases the student understanding and pleasure, bound to an art serving a public good. Self-evidently, art activity contractually in education has to be of service to society. I have laboured the point that the original capacity of art activity has always been to reflect, maintain, admit, provoke and self-realise, in a concept-idea, performance and spontaneously self-determined manner, an aspect of the social context of life in refined imaginative ways. The common cliché we might hear is the remark that art education is all about freedom and liberty simply confounds what we can be insensitive to and withdraws us from, the absent notion of good influence that can come from reading, for example, *Holes* by Louis Sachar.

I have explored how art education commonly works in teaching learner-like class situations and how this is in accordance with the process of welfare maximization overall. Teaching standards in art education relate to the curriculum requirements of art and professional standards of teaching in general. Everyone knows in art education that students' perceptions, cognitions, feelings and actions affect the production-performance of the art, based on the methods, the thinking, the ideas and the inventiveness of how commonly the student expresses the higher qualities of an art's content conjoined to experiences that involve welfare maximization overall requirements. Art education also satisfies welfare maximisation conditions because it commonly and ordinarily "gives special prominence to the more elevated experiences of human life" (Crisp, 1997, p. 25).

Why should art cultivation matter to us more than it currently does? As I have attempted to expound upon, art education forms part of the idea of welfare maximization overall related to the greatest happiness principle. An art education is an integral and vital part of this concern, which as Mill argued, helps the student to feel part of society and helps them adjust their minds conjoined to shedding light on the greatest happiness principle. Our human happiness, common to all in society, involves art education with its intellectual, moral, social and sympathetic feelings of life giving rise more substantially to certain claims of insight that our human happiness is intimately drawn towards. The formative arts, as Kant refers to them, "penetrates into the region of ideas" giving "a greater extension to the field of intuition than is open to others to do" (Kant, 1928, §. 53). Art education is taken up as a generative power of life forming plausible estimates of it, independent of common productions that can represent deeper meaning because of the individuality in it of particular things and universal claims. Hence, it is detrimental to human happiness overall if students are denied art education. Art education adds to our human happiness in intelligent, moral and social ways. This is Mill's proposition and that of many other renowned theorists that art education enables us to experience, realise, see, hear and contemplate convincing appeals of our causes of action in the world and our character of being in the world. It allows expression of all kinds of affections and intelligent and virtuous actions that correspondingly enable students to make improvements that can reciprocally affect ordinary life pleasures and understanding of our world.

With realistic goals of achievement in an art educational lesson, having typical notions, features and concerns manifesting moral, social, intellectual and human sympathetic feelings through undertaking a structured ranged of developmental exercises, art education can reflect acutely, students' awareness of their world, themselves, their culture and their social existence. There are, then, citizenship issues embedded in an art curriculum not least through sympathetic human feelings being expressed, examined and explored through literature, poetry, dance, acting and music, for example. Mill felt that art education represented part of our temperament and sensitivities of life. That art education enables us to know ourselves better, and in the process feel less helpless, foolish and pig-like.

In this work I have briefly stated what the normal student reaction experience can be like when they are taken to a Beethoven concert; the different imaginative configured drawings of an albatross that students are capable of producing which are right and appropriate to the art task and a notion of teaching of art responding to students' actual work that relate to understanding art concerns and life concerns linked to this task and what it can be like for students to read *Cinderella* where the reading activates realisations which extort delight, intensity and heightened awareness from them in proportion befitting the common comprehension and feelings of a young student expressing their solidarity with the story. I have spoken of Sibley's aesthetic concepts, of 'high art' and 'low art' difficulties, of 'higher qualities of art' and of how the game push-pin and poetry are not commensurate pleasures, and how things in education do not change because there are always thirteen year old students like Debbie to teach. Additionally, how this can bring out unequivocally the importance of good teaching in art education and the superior way art can bring out social issues involving Debbie, taken into account the ideas of Parsons and Blocker that "we understand people well only when we understand the assumptions they make".

From what has been said, a possible conception of Mill's thinking that we might view as correct is how higher art educational experiences are the enchantments we regularly desire and consistently adore when we are conscious of their disclosures that concomitantly makes recognisable our common sources of shared human sympathy due to the verdict of the art we have formed that may move us by association. However, we too often overlook in and out of the teaching profession the relevance of art education. Some mistakenly believe that art has little impact on life, that it has only immediate appeal, that it is not of the concrete, that it appears impractical, too subjective, that its pleasure is the same as any another pleasure, that it is too capricious, and that it is concerned with appearances and concepts that are of no necessity. I have presented adequate evidence in this body of work to refute many of these points of view. Art in education can express our true relationships to life as we experience it with the eminent respect shown for it.

An education system is only outstandingly useful, a utilitarian like Mill would argue, when in an agreed aesthetic, intellectual, moral, social and practical fashion, the higher outcomes of the greatest happiness principles of life of discerning enjoyments and keener sympathetic, common feelings that art education can command, with ideas and properties we can grasp in connection to justifying our associations to them, by what the art production-performance indicates. The habits, cultivations and actions that are the representative interests of all people with the general norms of life displayed in the art related to students' experiences endows the art production-performance with those anchors of life we desire and need.

Certainly there are various artistic, social and moral objections concerning welfare maximisation overall that have been legitimately raised by theorists and which continue to be raised. If art activity is only what the majority of people think it should be (but it might not be) when "all the forces of society act in one single direction" (Mill, 1897, p. 373), then the best beneficial means for promoting the ideas, actions, freedoms and qualities of life, may become, as Mill suggests, problematic? The majority of people in society may think, contrarily, however, in terms of a plurality manifesting an attitude and a feeling of mind in agreement with the art object. People who differ in their understanding about art education and the world can, therefore, come to a consensus about standards of welfare maximisation overall that flow from definite concepts, shared ideas and collective reasons justifying and extracting from an art what art education can contribute to society. For art education to justify itself, this would mean a uniformed, sustained and habitual higher order of diverse art activities-experiences which can be measured for effect through educational, humanistic and scientific ways understanding art from what arises out of it, of important human admiration that the student can grasp, advancing the past, the present and the future in proportion to vigorous thoughts, concepts, activities and with reasons susceptible to the sensibilities and capabilities of students in art educational situations.

I have stressed that the higher pleasures of life are part-and-parcel of the common happiness conditions of a flourishing society. To draw from such pleasures universally means being able to derive from one's own experiences and from other individuals their experiences, one's own interests and concerns tempered by respect for everyone in life, with different opinions coming together harmoniously to benefit from different conceptions of art activity in education, of each other's concerns through common shared life experiences. Many novels and poems, for example, illustrate the sphere of our thoughts and feelings amid the pleasures and the pains we experience. The pedagogy of teaching art uses our perceptions, cognitions, feelings and actions conjoined to ideas, properties and concepts in purposeful practical standard ways as I have elucidated.

The tenet of Mill's aesthetic art thinking was that art educational experiences ought to assimilate the scenery of life that is susceptible to student embodied experiences, possessing the higher qualities of life entwined in community values, for the habitual associations of culture for finer common living in the world. For Mill, the higher qualities are what open up and penetrate new possibilities that succeed with continuity and change, that self-maintain and strengthen the greatest happiness for all people. Why Mill felt that art education requires superior, aesthetic, human outlooks was to be able to estimate pain and pleasure appropriately, admitting what we agree about in the capable, probable, realistic, deductive and impressionable confirming claims of such experiences as I have briefly alluded to in reference to Aristotle's *Poetics*. Furthermore, for welfare maximisation overall to work, Mill recognised that frequent practice, discussion and opportunity to experience the benefits of art education would be required in order to grasp developmentally the rising standards for higher qualities of life to be experienced and expressed. But in a lot of schools frequent practice, discussion and opportunity in art is not provided. What are we forfeiting then relating to what art activity can reveal, redeem and enlarge that is good for us?

We need to facilitate the students' confidence to perform, realise, widen and deepen their execution of a work of art through the various forms of art in: drama, music, poetry, literature, dance, fashion, crafts, design, architecture, sculpture and painting, for example. Art education is not to shut out from view the warmest feelings and thoughts of students corresponding to understanding art in appearance, of what is brought home to them through art educational engagement in sensitive ways, the excitement and the movements that shape great human productions, actions and sympathies with relevance and meaning for us all. In unique ways, art in education serves to elucidate life's social common experiences. Art education along these lines is representing the concerns of welfare maximisation overall. So why is it that we constantly fail to understand the importance of art education? Art activity and experience offers what no other subject is capable of ever achieving. For many theorists, life receives from art not merely productions reflecting, for example, a man or a woman in the world but a man and woman refined, with faults and failures that can enlarge our cognition conjoined to any number of representations of how astonishing, horrible, admirable and hard working people are. Mill believed that aesthetic education was the equal to moral and intellectual education and connected to them interconnectedly. Communicating our feelings, desires, needs, thoughts, reflections and imagination that gives us pleasure, that begets our spirit in social ways, can show itself to full advantage in art education. Performances and productions of art in learner-like educational situations can render conceptions, ideas and experiences of life that are lacking from other subjects. Art education, when commonly and normatively taught, touches everyone deeply, producing an expansion of student contemplation connected to the surprises and distinctions of the art revealing conceptions of existence that are appealing to us as a consequence of its own account.

A further point of difference about art education is the way commonality, familiarity and the ordinariness of our experiences in art activity exercises can stretch considerably via adequate, pedagogical input the estimates attracting and directing the student's cognition, movement, feelings, actions and sensations in ways that enable the students en masse to express sentiments closer to their lives in imaginative, kindred, animating presentations. It is not the unintelligent, shallow, dull and morally repugnant impressions that get expressed in art education but rather the consciousness of things that in free, roving and thoughtful ways represent richly, deservedly and cherishingly some of our most happy and trusted iron clad feelings. We admire the child who dances, who paints, who plays music, who writes a poem and who in a school's play is one of the actors on stage, but we do not take seriously enough what is occurring in these instances, of how art experience enriches life.

In the practical aspects that can engulf us, we put to one side our aesthetic life. The natural affect of our aesthetic experiences, which Mill thought should play a part in the practical, as a critical difference to be used to affect our reasoning, passes us by unrecognized. In such moments, practical considerations can drown out everything else, our minds shrinks, the music stops and we forget that art education is part of a higher culture of life. Mechanical actions rightly may not need art aesthetic experience but life morally, socially, intellectually and sympathetically certainly does.

So the problem with educating students with little art educational experience is, as Kant indicates, how are we to remember our pleasures of a fair summer's day, of mother giving me a kiss on my cheeks, of my dad taking me to a football game and the dress that my aunty bought me? Who does not find some deliverance from reading a novel, going to the ballet, making a chair out of oak having visited the Grand Canyon on a school trip or being taken to a local photography-craft exhibition in town? What stirs up a crowd of sensations for the purpose that enables me to describe "a beautiful morning: The sun arose, as out of virtue rises peace" (Kant, 1928, §. 49) or the lines "I remember, I remember, the house where I was born…(Thomas Hood, 1799–1845), or equally "The old Lie: Dulce et decorum est, Pro patria mori" (Wilfred Owen, 1893–1918). The students' imagination can express what is prompting and transforming their art work through the impulses, transitions and actions produced by the rhythms, tempo, reverie experience and laments shaped by the poetry, music, drama, painting, and film exercises, for example. An immense variety of romantic, surreal, conceptual, representational, symbolist, aboriginal and abstract art thinking, for example, can convey information for the purpose of cherishing an interest in the object of art with understanding and agreement about the art which can lift the spirit. The invigorating, significant, not to be forgotten incidents that are important delights in themselves of the art we experience are often part of life's common existance that can fortify our wellbeing in a manner that benefits other meditations on life, helping us to solve other problems. Art productions, in their own right, produce scenes, incidents, evocations and events of imagined and real-like thought connections to do with this or that character, involving our intercourse with the world and its reflections, of how we experience our existence, see it and feel it. Art production, Kant surmises, can "diffuse in the mind a multitude of sublime and tranquillizing feelings, and gives a boundless outlook into a happy future" (Kant, 1928, §. 49) or indeed the reverse as Aristotle mentions in his *Poetics*.

When we enter an art classroom we might stumble upon what looks like on first view, scraps of painted paper sheets, an assortment of left over fabrics half stitched together seemingly with no structure, pieces of foam board and acrylic lying on a student table, a few rough poetical lines in an exercise book, a drum beat that has not got the rhythm right, a dance movement not extending itself sufficiently in a certain direction, a voice not always in tune with the music. A teacher of art will look upon these incidents not as chaotic states but rather as containing common ways for discovering qualities of an art beginning to show a superiority of thought and action within such fragments that have been selected. The main benefits of an art education consist, as remarked, of common ground experiences of life. As instances that when looked upon and heard are valid because they retain, explore and embody with reality our moral, intellectual, aesthetic and social alliances representing our social spirit and our social unity with the personality, character, feeling, effervescence and intimation that belong to each students' own impulse. We become inspired, grateful and moved by the acting capacities that children bring to our lives, by the music we listen to, by the plays we go and see and by the poems and novels we read, for example. In spontaneous, imaginative, idea based and techne ways, art in education, as surmised, reflects our laughter, innocence, fragility, delicateness, colourfulness, brightness, modesty, humbleness, quietness, shyness, excitation and vitality. Concerned with the familiar and the ordinary, art education binds those ties that we share, in act-like concord ways, through the refined powers of art activity and experience with its aesthetic, moral, social and intellectual consciousness of an alliance that can bring more earthy substance that can indispensably and felicitously affect some of the proper forces for living well in life.

A school without art education is a school without a soul and without a balance to it. Art in education is a resource that we should be more indebted to as it can preserve and nourish so much goodness in the world. Recognizing that art activity is a place where students can express their fancies, sensuous, delightful, pleasurable, compulsive, emotional and precious creative ideas communicating just what our human relationships are without ever subordinating our reasoning and our understanding. By celebrating community culture through different kinds of human enjoyment, excitement, discontent, exuberance and thoughtful cognition via teaching instruction, critical teaching judgements and educational standards of life, student art productions become meaningfully presented. It seems to me that the very best of art in the world past and present entertains such feelings and thoughts deeply. If we throw all this potential goodness away, if we take it all for granted as insignificant, if we pretend that it is unimportant in education and if we are not particular clever at translating teaching art standards into pedagogical practices above testing and constant inspections, comprehending, arising and being enriched by art, the quality of our human happiness, our pleasures in life, our social unity and our moral and intellectual capacities will not derive sufficient higher aesthetic, intellectual, social and moral real joy for a prosperous balance of mind that is the premised idea, however faulty, that is part of welfare maximisation overall. Art education is no push-pin consciousness of life. We should accept the irrefutable premise that art education should be more interwoven into the fabric of our educational system.

REFERENCES

Arbuthnot, M. H. (1959). *Time for poetry: A teacher's anthology.* Toronto, ON: Scott Foresman and Company.

Associated Board of the Royal School of Music. (2014). *Making music: Teaching, learning & playing in the UK.* Retrieved from http://network.youthmusic.org.uk/sites/default/files/research/2014_Making_Music_web_version_0.pdf

Astley, N. (Ed.). (2002). *Staying alive: Real poems for unreal times.* Northumberland, England: Bloodaxe Books.

Auden, W. H. (1979). Writing. In R. Gibbons (Ed.), *The poet's work: 29 masters of 20th century poetry on the origins and practice of their art* (pp. 184–190). Boston, MA: Houghton Mifflin Company.

Batistatou, A., Doulis E. A., Tiniakos, D., Anogiannaki, A., & Charalabopoulos, K. (2010). The introduction of medical humanities in the undergraduate curriculum of Greek medical schools: Challenge and necessity. *Hippokratia, 14*(4), 241–243.

Berlin, I. (1998). *The proper study of mankind: An anthology of essays.* New York, NY: Farrar, Straus and Giroux.

Blackburn, S. (2001). *Being good: An introduction to ethics.* Oxford, England: Oxford University Press.

Burckhardt, J. (1987). In P. Murray (Ed.), *The architecture of the Italian renaissance.* Middlesex, England: Penguin Books.

Carroll, N. (2005). Dance. In J. Levinson (Ed.), *The Oxford handbook of aesthetics.* Oxford, England: Oxford University Press.

Comte-Sponville, A. (2005). *The little book of philosophy* (F. Wynne, Trans.). London, England: Vintage.

Crisp, R. (1997). *Mill on utilitarianism.* London, England: Routledge.

Croce, B. (1968). *Aesthetic* (D. Ainslie, Trans.). New York, NY: The Noonday Press.

Danto, A. C. (1981). *The transfiguration of the commonplace: A philosophy of art.* Cambridge, MA: Harvard University Press.

Dewey, J. (1944). *Democracy and education.* New York, NY: The Free Press.

Dewey, J. (1974). Human nature and conduct. In R. D. Archambault (Ed.), *John Dewey on education: Selected writings.* Chicago, IL: University of Chicago Press.

Dewey, J. (1980). *Art as experience.* New York, NY: Perigree Books.

Dickens, C. (1989). *Hard times.* Oxford, England: Oxford University Press.

Eaton, M. M. (1995). The social construction of aesthetic response. *British Journal of Aesthetics, 35*(2), 95–106.

Efland, A. (1990). *A history of art education: Intellectual and social currents in teaching the visual arts.* New York, NY: Teachers College Press.

Eisner, E. (2005). *Reimagining schools: The selected works of Elliot W. Eisner.* London, England: Routledge.

Gaut, B. (2007). *Art, emotion and ethics.* Oxford, England: Oxford University Press.

Gombrich, E. (1960). *Art and illusion; A study in the psychology of pictorial representation.* London, England: Phaidon Press.

Gordon J. (2005). Medical humanities: To cure sometimes, to relieve often, to comfort always. *Medical Journal of Australia, 182*(1), 5–8.

Graham, G. (1995). Learning from art. *British Journal of Aesthetics, 35*(1), 26–37.

Greene, M. (1995). *Releasing the imagination: Essays on education, the arts, and social change.* San Francisco, CA: Jossey-Bass.

Halliwell, S. (1998). *Aristotle's poetics.* London, England: Gerald Duckworth and Co. Ltd.

Hegel G. W. F. (1988). *Hegel's aesthetics: Lectures on fine art* (Vol. 1, T. M. Knox, Trans.). Oxford, England: Clarendon Press.

Hegel G. W. F. (1993). In M. Inwood (Ed.), *Introductory lectures on aesthetics* (B. Bosanquet, Trans.). London, England: Penguin Books.

REFERENCES

Heidegger, M. (1993). The origin of the work of art. In D. F. Krell (Ed.), *Basic writings*. London, England: Routledge.

Herbert, Z. (1985). *Barbarian in the garden* (M. March & J. Anders, Trans.). London, England: A Harvest Book, Harcourt Brace & Company.

Hughes, T., & Godwin, F. (1979). *Elmet*. London, England: Faber & Faber.

Hume, D. (1965). In J. Lenz (Ed.), *Of the standard of taste, and other essays*. Indianapolis, IN: Bobbs-Merrill.

Hyman, J. (2006). *The objective eye color, form, and reality in the theory of art*. Chicago, IL: University of Chicago Press.

Johannessen, K. S. (2004). Wittgenstein and the aesthetic domain. In P. B. Lewis (Ed.), *Wittgenstein, aesthetic and philosophy*. Aldershot, England: Ashgate Publishing Limited.

Kant, I. (1928). *The critique of judgment* (J. C. Meredith, Trans.). Oxford, England: Clarendon Press.

Kendall, R. (Ed.). (1988). *Cézanne by himself*. London, England: Macdonald and Co. Ltd.

Keyte, H., & Parrott, A. (1984). Notes accompanying CD. *On Taverner Consort, Monteverdi: Vespro della beata vergine (1610)*. Hayes, England: EMI Records Ltd.

Kierkegaard, S. (1987). The tragic in ancient drama, reflected in the tragic in modern drama. In H. V. Hong & E. H. Hong (Eds.), *Either/Or, Part 1*. Princeton, NJ: Princeton University Press.

Klee, P. (1953). *Pedagogical sketchbook* (S. Moholy-Nagy, Trans.). London, England: Faber and Faber.

Küng, H. (1981). *Art and the question of meaning*. (E. Quinn, Trans.). New York, NY: The Crossroad Publishing Company.

Leddy, T. (2001). The red dust. *British Journal of Aesthetics, 41*(2), 207–221.

Levinson, J. (1996). *The pleasures of aesthetics: Philosophical essays*. Ithaca, NY: Cornell University Press.

Lowenfeld, V., & Brittain, W. L. (1987). *Creative and mental growth*. Upper Saddle River, NJ: Prentice Hall.

MacIntyre, A. (2002). *A short history of ethics*. London, England: Routledge.

Malraux, A. (1978). *The voices of silence* (S. Gilbert, Trans.). Princeton, NJ: Princeton University Press.

Merleau-Ponty, M. (1964). Eye and mind. In J. Wild (Ed.), *The primacy of perception*. Evanston, IL: Northwestern University Press.

Midgley, M. (2014). *Are you an illusion?*. Durham, England: Acumen Publishing.

Mill, J. S. (1897). In J. W. Gibbs (Ed.), *Early essays*. London, England: George Bell and Sons.

Mill, J. S. (1980). *Mill on Bentham and Coleridge*. Cambridge, England: Cambridge University Press.

Mill, J. S. (1985). *On liberty*. London, England: Penguin Books.

Mill, J. S. (2007). *Utilitarianism*. New York, NY: Dover Publications.

Mill, J. S. (2008). *Autobiography*. Rockville, MD: Arc Manor.

Moore, G. E. (1988). *Principia ethica*. Buffalo, NY: Prometheus Books.

Moore, H., & Hedgecoe, J. (1986). *Henry Moore: My ideas, inspiration and life as an artist*. London, England: Ebury Press.

Morris, W. (1979). In A. L. Morton (Ed.), *Political writings of William Morris*. London, England: Lawrence & Wishart.

Murdoch, I. (1993). *Metaphysics as a guide to morals*. London, England: Penguin Books.

Murdoch, I. (1997). The sovereignty of good over other concepts. In R. Crisp & M.Slote (Eds.), *Virtue ethics* (pp. 99–117). Oxford, England: Oxford University Press.

National Society for Education in Art and Design. (2014). *NSEAD art, craft and design educator survey report*. Retrieved from http://www.nsead.org/Downloads/NSEAD_ART_CRAFT_AND_DESIGN_EDUCATOR_SURVEY_REPORT_2014.pdf

Nehamas, A. (2007). *Only a promise of happiness: The place of beauty in a world of art*. Princeton, NJ: Princeton University Press.

Nietzsche, F. (1968). In W. Kaufmann (Ed.), *The will to power* (W. Kaufmann & R. J. Hollingdale, Trans.). New York, NY: Vintage Books.

Nietzsche, F. (1969). *On the genealogy of morals and ecco homo* (W. Kaufmann, Trans.). New York, NY: Vintage Books.

Noddings, N. (2005). *Happiness and education*. Cambridge, England: Cambridge University Press.

Nussbaum, M. (1986). *The fragility of goodness: Luck and ethics in Greek tragedy and philosophy*. Cambridge, England: Cambridge University Press.

Nussbaum, M. (1990). *Love's knowledge: Essays on philosophy and literature*. Oxford, England: Oxford University Press.

Parsons, M. J. (1987). *How we understand art: A cognitive developmental account of aesthetic experience*. Cambridge, England: Cambridge University Press.

Parsons, M. J., & Blocker, H. G. (1993). *Aesthetics and education*. Urbana, IL: University of Illinois Press.

Plato. (1997). Republic. In J. M. Cooper (Ed.), *Complete works*. Indianapolis, IN: Hackett Publishing Company.

President's Committee on the Arts and the Humanities. (2011). *Reinvesting in arts education: Winning America's future through creative schools*. Retrieved from http://www.pcah.gov/sites/default/files/PCAH_Reinvesting_4web_0.pdf

Proust, M. (2001). *The complete short stories* (J. Neugroschel, Trans.). New York, NY: Copper Square Press.

Rancière, J. (2009). *Aesthetics and its discontents*. Cambridge, England: Polity Press.

Reid, L. A. (1986). The conceptual understanding of art and the aesthetic; their importance for education. In A. Dyson (Ed.), *Art and design education: Heritage and prospect, Bedford Way papers 14*. London, England: Institute of Education, University of London.

Richardson, M. E. (1948). *Art & the child*. London, England: University of London Press.

Rogers, M. R. (1984). *Teaching approaches in music theory*. Carbondale and Edwardsville, IL: Southern Illinois University Press.

Ruskin, J. (1960). In J. G. Links (Ed.), *The stones of Venice*. New York, NY: Da Capo Press.

Sanders, A. (1986). Dickens and the English language. In I. C. B. Dear (Comp.), *Oxford English: A guide to language*. Oxford, England: Oxford University Press.

Schiller, F. (1967). In E. M. Wilkinson & L. A. Willoughby (Eds.), *On the aesthetic education of man: In a series of letters*. Oxford, England: Clarendon Press.

Schopenhauer, A. (1995). In D. Berman (Ed.), *World as will and idea* (J. Berman, Trans.). London, England: Orion Publishing Group.

Sibley, F. (2004). Aesthetic concepts. In P. Lamarque & S. H. Olsen (Eds.), *Aesthetics and the philosophy of art: The analytic tradition*. Oxford, England: Blackwell Publishing.

Slote, M. (1998). Virtue ethics, utilitarianism, and symmetry. In R. Crisp (Ed.), *How should we live?*. Oxford, England: Clarendon Press.

Spender, S. (2000). My parents. In A. Warwick (Ed.), *The nation's favourite poems of childhood*. London, England: BBC Worldwide Ltd.

Storr, A. (1992). *Music and the mind*. New York, NY: Ballantine Books.

Thomas, D. (1979). Poetic manifesto. In R. Gibbons (Ed.), *The poet's work: 29 masters of 20th century poetry on the origins and practice of their art* (p. 184–190). Boston, MA: Houghton Mifflin Company.

Thoreau, H. D. (2009). In D. Searls (Ed.), *The Journal* (pp. 1837–1861). New York, NY: New York Review of Books.

Tolstoy, L. (1994). In W. G. Jones (Ed.), *What is art?* (A. Maude, Trans.). Bristol, England: Bristol Classical Press.

Whitman, W. (1986). In M. Crowley (Ed.), *Leaves of grass, the first 1855 edition*. London, England: Penguin Books.

Williams, B. (1997). Morality, the peculiar institution. In R. Crisp & M. Slote (Eds.), *Virtue ethics* (pp. 45–65). Oxford, England: Oxford University Press.

Wittgenstein, L. (1966). In C. Barrett (Ed.), *Lectures and conversations on aesthetics, psychology and religious beliefs*. Oxford, England: Basil Blackwell.

Wittgenstein, L. (1967). In G. E. M. Anscome & G. H. von Wright (Eds.), *Zettel* (G. E. M. Anscombe, Trans.). Oxford, England: Basil Blackwell.

Wittgenstein, L. (1969). In R. Rhees (Ed.), *The blue and brown books*. Oxford, England: Basil Blackwell.

Wittgenstein, L. (1980). In G. H. von Wright (Ed.), *Culture and value* (P. Winch, Trans.). Chicago, IL: The University of Chicago Press.

Wollheim, R. (1980). *Art and its objects*. Cambridge, England: Cambridge University Press.

Lightning Source UK Ltd.
Milton Keynes UK
UKOW06f2059130116

266374UK00006B/290/P

9 789463 000925